# THE PRINCE IN THE HEATHER

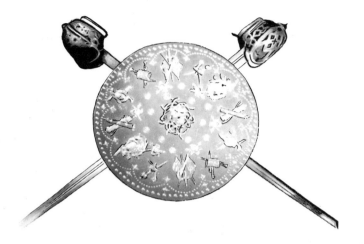

# THE PRINCE
# IN THE HEATHER

*by*

## ERIC LINKLATER

*Photographs by Don Kelly*

HODDER AND STOUGHTON

The Publishers gratefully acknowledge the help that The
Drambuie Liqueur Co Ltd has generously given in the
publication of this book

Printed in Scotland for Hodder & Stoughton Ltd, St. Paul's
House, Warwick Lane, London, E.C.4 by
Thomas Nelson (Printers) Ltd, London and Edinburgh

*Loch nan Uamh: the Beginning and
the End*

# I

CHARLES EDWARD LOUIS PHILIPPE CASIMIR STUART, known to historians as the Young Pretender and to romantics as Bonnie Prince Charlie, was born in Rome on the 20th December, 1720, the son of James Francis Edward Stuart and the Princess Clementina Sobieska of Poland, a daughter of the great John Sobieski who saved Europe from the Turks. James Edward Stuart, the Old Pretender, was the only surviving son of James II, King of England, Scotland, and Ireland, who died in 1701. After his death James Edward was acclaimed as James III by his Jacobite adherents and Louis XIV of France. Almost the whole of his life was spent in exile, in France or Italy, and three attempts to re-capture his lost throne were defeated. In 1745 a fourth attempt was led by Charles Edward.

Clever, handsome, and gay, the Prince had seen action at the siege of Gaeta when he was only fourteen, and acquired a liberal education from two tutors, one Protestant and the other Catholic. He was devoted to music, and trained his body for endurance by strenuous exercise. At the age of twenty-four his ambition to regain his father's kingdom was encouraged by Louis XV of France: France being again at war with England, whose Hanoverian monarch, George II, had lately commanded an Anglo-Hanoverian army at the battle of Dettingen. At Dunkirk preparation was made for an invasion of England, but a gale wrecked or seriously damaged the French transports, and French enthusiasm dissolved. The Prince, however, was undismayed. He wrote to his father that he had 'taken a firm resolution to conquer or to die', and with the help of some private friends eventually reached the west coast of Scotland in the armed brig *Doutelle*. With a few companions he landed in Loch nan Uamh, between Moidart and Arisaig, on the 25th July, 1745.

On the 19th August he raised his standard at Glenfinnan, at the head of Loch Shiel, and with a gradually increasing Highland army—the nucleus consisted of Macdonalds of Clanranald and Keppoch, and Lochiel's Camerons—he marched on Edinburgh. The capital, panic-stricken, offered no resistance, but the Castle was held against him. At

Prestonpans a Hanoverian army under Sir John Cope was routed after seven minutes of furious fighting, and by the beginning of November the Prince had begun his march on London at the head of an army that probably numbered about 5,000 foot and 600 horse.

The apparent recklessness of the advance was palliated by knowledge of the large number of people, in England and Wales, who professed their detestation of the Hanoverian king and their sympathy with the Jacobite cause. In several parts of the country there were Jacobite clubs whose members made a practice of drinking the health of 'the king over the water', and as evidence of their apparent loyalty to the Pretender there still survive many of the elegantly engraved glasses from which they drank with enthusiasm their treasonable toast. The glasses were handsome enough—delicately or flamboyantly inscribed with Stuart emblems—but the hands which raised them preferred crystal to steel, and when the Prince came into England the drinking Jacobites, or all but a handful, stayed at home.

Through Carlisle and Manchester the Highland army advanced, over roads deep in snow, and on the 4th December reached Derby. The young Duke of Cumberland, was by then commanding an army of 12,000 at Lichfield; General Wade had an army some fifteen miles west of York; and a large army of 30,000 men lay at Finchley to defend London. When Lord George Murray, the Prince's lieutenant-general, and others in the Highland army counselled prudence and retreat, they had cogent arguments but may have lacked the Prince's intuition. He was intent on maintaining the advance, and it is just possible that audacity would have been rewarded; for London was in a state of panic, as Edinburgh had been, the army at Finchley was a mere rabble, and had they been given more time the Welsh Jacobites might have marched. But the Prince was over-ruled, and the Highlanders returned miserably to Scotland.

In January they won a small, ragged, inconclusive victory at Falkirk, but Lord George Murray's authority prevailed over much dissension and the retreat was continued to Inverness. Cumberland took command of a

*Jacobite Wine-glass: an Instrument of Treason*

Hanoverian army in the north, and by the end of February, 1746, was in Aberdeen where he remained till the beginning of April. When he advanced towards Inverness he moved rapidly, and the Jacobite army, mustered in great haste, occupied a position of indifferent advantage on Culloden Moor, the Prince making his headquarters at Culloden House, the home of Duncan Forbes, Lord President of the Court of Session. Rations were short, the men hungry, but a rash attempt was made to surprise Cumberland, in camp near Nairn, by a night-march. The Highland army was not trained for so difficult an exercise, there may have been some loss of direction, and at the uncomfortable hour of two o'clock in the morning the order was given to retire; Lord George Murray was again the advocate of caution, and Lochiel supported him. Hungry, tired, and disappointed, the army returned to Culloden Moor and got there about six o'clock; but there were many stragglers.

The 16th April was a day of bitter cold with a north-easterly gale that carried rain and sleet. The Jacobite army numbered some 5,000 men, the Hanoverian about 9,000. The Hanoverians were better drilled, better taught, and very much stronger in artillery. The battle began about one o'clock, when the armies stood four or five hundred yards apart, and was over before two. Cumberland's tactical management of his army was sound, and only on his extreme left did the Highland charge break his front. The Jacobite army was defeated by the overwhelming superiority of their enemy's well-controlled and effectively directed fire-power. The Duke of Cumberland might have lived to enjoy much honour from his victory, but blackened his name by the foul and insensate cruelty with which he followed it. No quarter was given, wounded and prisoners were killed, and his soldiers' atrocious behaviour on the field and in the immediate pursuit was only a prelude to his merciless persecution of the Highlands.

The Prince stayed till all hope had clearly gone, then with a little party about him rode to the farm of Balvraid. He waited there for a short time, but it was perilous to linger, and his long flight began.

*On Culloden Moor*

# II

WHAT follows—in these pages, that is—will be, in the main, an account of the ardours and endurances, the alarms and circumstances of the Prince's flight throughout the five months of relentless pursuit that he at last evaded by his own fortitude and the unfailing devotion of his Highland friends. But lightly overlaid on that, the real story, will be occasional reference to a more recent journey over the route of the flight, the purpose of which was to compose a documentary film that would illustrate the story; and this modern addition is made because it conveniently allows some description of those Highland parts and Hebridean islands of Scotland through which Charles Edward fled, and which are still accessible only to the old-fashioned conveyance of walking-boots and small boats. The Highlands and Islands are, as they say, still 'unspoiled'; which means that they have not yet been turned into areas of industrial production or suburban development, but largely remain as they were in the Prince's time, with the laudable addition of a few good roads that allow easy transit from one side of the country to the other.

For this intrusion of the present into the past I apologise, and shall restrict it to a minimum. But that minimum may help the romantic traveller—and romanticism of this sort is an honest emotion—to follow as much of Prince Charlie's route as may give him, or her, an impression of what occurred in those desperate months when a reckless but valiant young man, who brought great misery to his own people, created a legend of courage in adversity and a simple loyalty impervious to savage menace or lavish bribery, that still sheds a light of wild-seeming but true nobility on the grim heights that reach from Loch Arkaig to dark Loch Hourn, on the silver beaches of Morar, and the storm-swept, desolate beauty of the Outer Isles. What follows will be a sober account of profitless but memorable heroism, glossed by some relevant information about the contemporary scene.

*The White Sands of Morar*

O N high ground overlooking the Moray Firth, the battlefield of
Culloden lies some four or five miles east of Inverness, and is now
the property of the National Trust for Scotland. Extensive tree-planting
has disguised the open moorland of 1746; it is traversed by a main road,
and its bleak exposure is mollified by sheltering pine-woods. Rude
gravestones mark the burial-place of dead clansmen—Camerons and
Stewarts of Appin, Macintoshes and Clan Donald, Frasers, Macleans,
and many others—and a great boulder called the Cumberland Stone
may be the vantage-point from which that bloodthirsty young man
watched the battle; it lasted no more than half an hour.

Later in the century Culloden House, where the Prince had spent
some time, sleeping with his boots on, was burnt; and then re-built to
a design of classical elegance. After the battle eighteen Jacobite officers,
all wounded, took refuge in the old house and for two days, their
wounds untended, lay in pain; then they were taken out to be shot.
One of them, a Fraser of the Master of Lovat's regiment, escaped the
slaughter; the others were buried at the edge of the domestic park.

Early in the afternoon of the 16th April the Prince rode in a southerly
direction to the ford of Faillie on the river Nairn, where General Wade's
military road from Inverness to Carrbridge crossed the river; and thence
down Strathnairn to Stratherrick, by Aberarder south of Loch Ruthven
and Farraline beside Loch Mhor, to Gortleck at its southern end. Here
was a house belonging to a kinsman of Lord Lovat, and there the Prince
met that most enigmatic of Highland chiefs whom Hogarth later drew
when Lovat was on his way to execution; and what Hogarth drew was
a greedy but otherwise inscrutable plump bonhomie. Lovat had sent his
son to join the Prince, but himself had prudently remained at home;
and now his hospitality was curt and limited. Someone has recorded that
Charles Edward was welcomed with a glass of wine, and sent on his
way after two more.

With him, when he left the battlefield, were Lord Elcho, who had
commanded his few Life Guards; his A.D.C., Alexander Macleod;

*Culloden : Grave of Clan Mackintosh*

Sheridan, his old tutor; the Irish soldier of fortune, Captain O'Sullivan; O'Neil, another Irishman; and Ned Burke who, despite his Irish name, had been born in North Uist and whose humble occupation was to carry one end of a sedan-chair in Edinburgh. He proved a stout-hearted and useful guide. Not all of them may have gone as far as Gortleck. The battle had come so suddenly to an end that no certain orders had been given for a rendezvous, and while some expected the remnants of the defeated army to re-assemble at Fort Augustus, more went hopefully to a meeting-place at Ruthven near Kingussie. The Prince wrote to Cluny Macpherson that night, and it is possible that he sent other messengers to try and repair confusion.

News of approaching dragoons sent him in a hurry from Gortleck, and he went by the Wade road to Fort Augustus, and south again by the river Oich—where now the Caledonian Canal joins Loch Oich and Loch Ness—as far as Invergarry castle; which was burnt by Cumberland, but its gaunt ruin remains. It was early morning on the 17th when he reached the empty castle, and somewhere near it Ned Burke found a stake-net in which were two salmon. These were boiled, and an oat-cake completed the meal. Either at Invergarry or the house of Droynachan, not far away, the Prince stayed till three o'clock in the afternoon, and then rode on down the north-west side of Loch Lochy—where the hills rise dark and steeply from the waters of the loch to bare heights of two or three thousand feet—and turned west to Loch Arkaig.

Here is an avenue of tall trees called the Dark Mile, and south of the little river Arkaig stands Achnacarry House, the home of Cameron of Lochiel. The old house was burnt in 1746, and in April of that year the 'gentle Lochiel' who had been almost the first to join the Prince lay helpless, having been wounded in both legs at Culloden. Loch Arkaig, a narrow water some twelve miles long, is well wooded at its eastern end, but to the west lies between bare and formidable hills that on the north rise to nearly three thousand feet, to more than that on the south. A rough path leads along the north shore to Kinloch Arkaig at the east

*Wade bridge at Faillie near Inverness*

end of Glen Pean, and there stood a cottage belonging to Donald Cameron of Glen Pean where, according to tradition, the Prince spent the night with a party now reduced to three: O'Sullivan, Father Allan Macdonald, and Ned Burke.

Till the late afternoon of the 18th he waited there for news, and it was then, perhaps, that he got from Lord George Murray a letter reproaching him for starting the adventure so recklessly, and offering, in conclusion, the resignation of his commission.

Murray's letter, written from Ruthven the day after the battle, opens on a chord of insufferable pomposity: 'As no person in these kingdomes ventured more franckly in the cause than myself and as I had more at stake than almost all the others put together, so to be sure I cannot but be very deeply affected with our late loss and present situation, but I declare that were your R.H. person in safety, the loss of the cause and the misfortunate and unhappy situation of my countrymen is the only thing that grieves me, for I thank God, I have resolution to bear my own and family's ruine without a grudge.'

He then makes the following accusation: 'It was highly wrong to have set up the royal standard without having positive assurance from his most Christian majesty that he would assist you with all his force, and as your royal family lost the crown of these realms upon the account of France, the world did and had reason to expect that France would seize the first favourable opportunity to restore your August family.'

For defeat at Culloden he blames the Prince and the Irishman O'Sullivan: O'Sullivan for incompetence, the Prince for giving him unwarranted responsibility. He adds, with a very pretty sneer, 'I wish Mr. O'Sulivan had never got any other charge in the Army than the care of the bagage which I have been told he had been brought up to and understood.'

With greater justification he denounces the incompetence of John Hay of Restalrig who was in charge of the commissariat: 'Mr. Hay

*Loch Garry*

whom Y.R.H. trusted with the principal direction of ordering provisions of late and without whose orders a boll of meal or farthing of monie was not to be delivered, has served Y.R.H. egregiously ill, when I spoke to him, he told me, the thing is ordered, it will be got etc. but he neglected his duty to such a degree that our ruin might probably been prevented had he done his duty: in short the three last days which were so critical our army was starved. This was the reason our night march was rendered abortive when we possibly might have surprised and defeated the enemy at Nairn, but for want of provisions a third of the army scattered to Inverness and the others who marched had not spirits to make it so quick as was necessary being really faint for want of provisions.'—The accuracy of this charge seems indisputable, for on the day before the battle the soldiers got only one biscuit apiece, and the abortive night attack may have been much weakened by the fact that many were foraging for themselves.

The letter then reaches its conclusion: 'Y.R.H. knows I always told I had no design to continue in the army: I would of late when I came last from Atholl have resigned my commission, but all my friends told me it might be of prejudice to the cause at such a critical time. I hope your R.H. will now accept my demission.'

It may well have been this letter which determined the Prince's subsequent movement and planted in his mind the idea of returning to France. Two days before his A.D.C., Alexander Macleod, had written to Cluny: 'We have suffered a good deal; but hope we shall soon pay Cumberland in his own Coin. We are to review to-morrow at Fort Augustus the Frasers, Camerons, Stewarts, Clanronalds, and Keppoch's people. His R.H. expects your people will be with us at furthest Friday morning. Dispatch is the more necessary that his Highness has something in view which will make an ample amends for this day's ruffle . . . For God's sake make haste to join us; and bring with you all the people can possibly be got together. Take care in particular of Lumisden and Sheridan, as they carry with them the Sinews of War.'

*Fashion in Mallaig: a fisherman*

Clearly when that was written he had no intention of leaving Scotland, and though he must have been disappointed by the failure of the clans to re-muster at Fort Augustus, there is nothing to suggest that he had lost hope. It is recorded indeed that here, in Glen Pean, with the braes of Morar before him, he ate with relish a simple meal of milk and curds, and was in good heart. But Murray's criticism could not be ignored—though often the Prince was to lay on him the blame for defeat—and if Murray thought Scotland could not be won without French help, then perhaps it would be prudent to go back to France and ask for help.

The braes of Morar lay ahead, and now the path was so rough that horses had to be left behind, and the Prince and his companions walked over the hills to the small glen of Meoble south of Loch Morar: a dozen miles or so, had the path been straight, but half as long again on broken ground. There are great hills on either side of the glen, and the waters of the loch are, in some parts, a thousand feet deep. Beyond the loch the narrow height of North Morar divides it from the yet grander Loch Nevis, and to the west the sea breaks on glittering white beaches.

For the better part of a day the Prince slept in a cottage in a wood, watched by Angus MacEachine, sometime surgeon in Glengarry's regiment and son-in-law of Angus MacDonald of Borradale; and at night, under a moon four days from the full, walked again to Borradale on the north shore of Loch nan Uamh, that opens off the Sound of Arisaig, where he had landed from the brig *Doutelle* just nine months before. He did not sleep in the house of Borradale, but in a cottage in a birch wood in nearby Glenbeasdale. Here he had a chance to recover from the fatigue of his flight, and enjoyed a little comfort. 'He was pretty well here,' says O'Sullivan. 'He had a little meal, lamb, butter; and straw to ly upon. He wanted it, for he had not eat a bit of bread since he supt at Ld. Lovets the night of the battle.' And from Borradale's wife he got a suit of clothes made in the Highland fashion.

At Borradale were several survivors of the battle, including young

*The rough road through Glen Pean*

Clanranald and Lord Elcho, and there was much debate about the wisdom of his going to look for a ship, or wait for a ship, in Skye or the Outer Isles. Young Clanranald thought he should stay in Arisaig, but now the Prince was intent on returning to France, and believed he could safely ask for help from the great lairds of Skye, MacDonald of Sleat and MacLeod of MacLeod. To his aid there came, instead of them, one of the best and sturdiest of all who gave him service, an old man of nearly seventy, by name Donald MacLeod, tenant of Gualtergill on Loch Dunvegan in Skye; and Donald was a seaman.

The Prince in his new tartan clothes met him among the birches of Glenbeasdale, and asked, 'Are you Donald MacLeod of Gualtergill in Skye?'—Their conversation is recorded in Donald's own narrative.

'Yes,' said Donald, 'I am the same man, may it please your Majesty, at your service. What is your pleasure wi' me?'

'Then,' said the Prince, 'you see, Donald, I am in distress. I therefore throw myself into your bosom, and let you do with me what you like. I hear you are an honest man, and fit to be trusted.'

In later years, when Donald told this story, the tears would run down his cheeks, and he would excuse them with 'Wha deel could help greeting when speaking on sic a sad subject?'—But to the Prince he replied, if his memory can be trusted: 'Alas, may it please your excellency, what can I do for you? For I am but a poor auld man, and can do very little for mysell.'

'Why,' said the Prince, 'the service I am to put you upon I know you can perform very well. It is that you may go with letters from me to Sir Alexander MacDonald and the Laird of MacLeod. I desire therefore to know if you will undertake this piece of service; for I am really convinced that these gentlemen for all that they have done, will do all in their power to protect me.'

At that Donald was greatly surprised—then grew indignant—and said plainly he would do nothing of the sort, though he should be hanged for refusing.

'What,' said he, 'does not your excellency know that these men have played the rogue to you altogether, and will you trust them for a' that? Na, you mauna do't.'

MacDonald and the Laird of MacLeod, he said, were even then searching for him, their militia combing the hills, and no farther away than ten or twelve miles across the sea. The sooner he left Arisaig the better, for at any moment they might put to sea and carry their search to the mainland. But unknown to Donald and the Prince there was a current rumour—which Cumberland believed—that already he had made good his escape and found a most unlikely refuge in faraway St. Kilda. All the available warships on the coast were ordered to go there, and with a considerable force of soldiers aboard they headed west into the Atlantic, and nearly frightened the poor St. Kildans out of their wits. Those simple islanders knew nothing of the Prince, and all they had lately heard from the outer world was a fanciful tale that the Laird of MacLeod had lately been at war 'with a great woman abroad', who presumably was Maria Theresa, Archduchess of Austria, Queen of Bohemia and Hungary; and MacLeod 'had got the better of her', though England was her ally.

This rumour, and the departure of the fleet, were of great service to the Prince, for the Long Island—all the Outer Isles, that is, from Barra to the Butt of Lewis—were now unguarded; and Donald was a good pilot who knew the Hebridean seas. When the Prince asked if he could find a boat to take him, not to Skye but to the farther isles, Donald promptly replied that he would do anything in the world to serve him, and he knew the very boat for the purpose. It was a boat that had belonged to a son of MacDonald of Borradale, a boy who had been killed at Culloden or butchered while he lay wounded; for nothing had been heard of him since the battle.

While Donald went to find the boat, the Prince wrote to Sheridan his old tutor—who had made his escape to France—and enclosed a letter to be shown to the Highland chiefs who had shared his campaign. 'When

25

I came into this Country,' he wrote, 'it was my only view to do all in my power for your good and safety. This I will allways do as long as life is in me. But alas! I see with grief, I can at present do little for you on this side the water, for the only thing that can now be done, is to defend your selves till the French assist you. If not, to be able to make better terms. To effectuate this, the only way is to assemble in a body as soon as possible, and then take measures for the best, which you that know the Country are only Judges of. This makes me be of little use here, whereas by my going into France instantly, however dangerous it be, I will certainly engage the French Court either to assist us effectually and powerfully, or at least to procure you such terms as you would not obtain otherways. My presence there, I flatter myself, will have more effect to bring this sooner to a determination than anybody else.'

Flatter himself he did, but perhaps excusably; and within a very short time his need of high hopes and an equal spirit became clear to all. It was a stoutly built, eight-oared boat that presently Donald brought for the voyage to the Outer Isles, and at nightfall on the 26th—two nights after the full moon—the Prince embarked with O'Sullivan, O'Neil, Father Allan MacDonald, Ned Burke, Donald MacLeod, and seven boatmen: one of whom was Donald's son, a boy of fifteen who had run away from the Grammar School of Inverness and provided himself with a claymore, dirk, and pistol to join the battle at Culloden.

It was against Donald's advice that they put to sea, for the old man foretold a gale of wind. He could see it coming. But the Prince was stubborn, he insisted on their sailing, and by the time they had rowed out of Loch nan Uamh into the Sound of Arisaig he regretted his decision; for the wind increased till a violent gale was blowing, with thunder, lightning, and heavy rain to add to their discomfort. Now the Prince demanded to be put ashore again. 'For,' said he, 'I had rather face cannons and muskets than be drowned in such a storm as this.'

But to turn back was impossible, for the shore of the Sound of Arisaig is dangerous ground, foul with reefs and half-tide rocks and broken water in which the boat would certainly have been lost. Their only hope was to find sea-room. 'Is it not as good for us to be drowned in clean water,' said Donald, 'as to be dashed in pieces on a rock and drowned too?'

So they turned the boat's head to steer north-west, and started their desperate voyage through the Cuillin Sound—Eigg, Rum, and Canna on their port side, the fierce coast of Skye to starboard—and so to Benbecula in the outer Hebrides. According to Captain Alexander MacDonald—of Clanranald's regiment, and later one of the Prince's companions in the Long Island—the wind was in the south-east, a 'violent tempest' he calls it; and by some mishap, as they rounded the point of Arisaig, the boat's bowsprit broke. From the point of Arisaig to Benbecula is all of seventy miles, but as the night was pitch-dark, they had no compass, and the wild gale blew till four hours after they landed, they may have sailed a longer course than that: Donald himself estimated it at thirty-two leagues. Though the boat is described as 'eight-oared' it is obvious, then, that after leaving Loch nan Uamh they hoisted sail, and running with the wind behind them made remarkable speed. For it was at 'peep of day,' says Donald, that they saw the coast of the Long Island.

Accounts of the voyage vary, and it is pretty clear that some of the passengers were so bewildered and bemused by the great heave and swirl of the high-running sea—now rearing white astern, now racing away under hissing foam—that they had very little notion of what was happening, and none at all of the quiet, seamanly skill of Donald and his crew. He himself says, 'After this'—after they had hoisted sail and headed north-west, that is—'all was hush and silence; not one word more among them'—the passengers, one may assume—'expecting every moment to be overwhelmed with the violence of the waves, and to sink down to the bottom.'

*The dancing coast at Elgol in Skye*

In a boat of that sort, in the middle years of the 18th century, there would probably be a mast stepped a little way forward of midships, and a loose-footed, square sail on a yard. In the 'hush and silence' Donald would sit down to leeward in the stern of the boat, with a long tiller over his shoulder, and on either side of the mast would be a man at the halliards to hoist the sail, or lower it, as need might require. There would be no words of command, because the men at the halliards would be seamen able to judge the speed of the boat, the devouring ferocity of the sea, and the compensating need to rise from a trough or go easily over a breaking crest. They had the additional fear, in the gross darkness of the night, of going ashore on Skye: a lee shore, if they were running north of their proper course, and the island full of militia-men too. More than once they may have had to luff and bear up into the wind when the roar of breakers under their lee warned them of danger. But Donald was a seaman, and rolling and lurching through the waves, with a wild spray breaking over them, he kept the boat alive; though the men who were bailing can have been the only ones who kept themselves warm.

On this painful and dangerous voyage the Prince would never admit that he was in distress, but 'bore up most surprisingly, and never wanted spirits.' This indeed is a tribute to his courage, for nothing leads more quickly to admission of defeat than sea-sickness, and there is no doubt that Charles was violently sick. He himself, says Donald, 'and all that were with him had reason to think that during the whole time the Prince was more or less under a bloody flux.' A haemorrhage is possible but improbable—its effect would have been debilitating, but once ashore the Prince showed no sign of weakness—and perhaps they mistook claret for blood.

The land that they saw ahead, when day broke, was Benbecula, between South Uist and North Uist, and with great difficulty—for the storm was still raging—they made a landing at Rossinish, and pulled their boat high up on the shore. There they went to a deserted hut, and made a fire to dry their clothes; for all were drenched to the skin. They spread their sail on the bare ground, and the Prince, well pleased with so much comfort, slept soundly. Donald had had the forethought to put an iron pot in the boat, and having caught a cow, they killed and but-chered it, and boiled beef in the pot. They stayed for two days and two nights in the hut at Rossinish.

*The eye of a conger*

TWO hundred and eighteen years later, the film-unit engaged to map and illustrate the Prince's flight chartered a boat in Mallaig to follow his path to the Long Island. Mallaig, a few miles north of Morar, on the southern horn of Loch Nevis, is a fishing-port whose houses, from the sea, appear to be haphazardly and a little precariously attached to a steep and sombre background; but its harbour is a robust and lively marine market, crowded with great, brown-varnished boats—broad in the beam, with a proudly rising sheer—that transfer their gleaming cargoes, among flocks of screaming sea-gulls, to lorries that nonchalantly manoeuvre on a slippery wooden pier. The chartered boat, called *Western Isles*, was a converted motor fishing-vessel, hardly different in appearance from her professional sisters, and on the first stage of her voyage she went out past Eigg and the cliffs of Rum to the shelter of an almost land-locked harbour on the south shore of Canna. She lay there over night, and in the morning continued her voyage to Loch Boisdale in South Uist.

From Loch Boisdale to Stornoway in Lewis is, in a straight line, more than eighty miles. The Prince landed on Benbecula on the 27th April, 1746, and for two months he moved erratically up and down the Long Island—nearly as far north as Stornoway, and as far south as Loch Boisdale—usually in vile discomfort, frequently hungry and often in danger, until on the 28th June he crossed to Skye in a very unconvincing disguise and the brave company of Flora MacDonald.

The film-unit in the *Western Isles* spent some days on the rugged east coast of the Long Island, and went ashore with its equipment at several places where the Prince had found rough and temporary refuge. The members of the unit discovered for themselves the inhospitable nature of the almost uninhabited shore, and in their search for true illustrations of the Prince's wandering were so fortunate as to experience bitter weather, hail showers, and strong winds, and the difficulty of landing from a small boat on steep, dark rocks carpeted with yellow sea-wrack.

They were nowhere exposed to danger or any grave discomfort,

*Mallaig: fish for sale*

but even to a meagre or slow imagination the possibility of danger on that wild coast or under the formidable cliffs of Skye was fairly obvious, and the certainty of extreme discomfort, during a long and enforced sojourn, was indisputable. The pictures recorded by their cameras reflect something of the scenery; and their minds were impressed with a new respect for the physical endurance and stout spirit of the Prince who, in smaller and less seaworthy boats than theirs, had created the excuse for their voyage.

*Eigg, Rum, and Blackface sheep*

IN the hut at Rossinish the Prince received a visit from old Clan-ranald, one of the great chiefs of Clan Donald, and though their conversation was not recorded, the gist of it can be inferred. On Monday, the 28th April, the Prince and his party put to sea again in the eight-oared boat, and now adopted new names. O'Sullivan posed as 'old Mr. Sinclair', the Prince as his son, and Father Allan MacDonald became Mr. Graham. Their destination was the island of Lewis, and before Clanranald left them the crew had been given instruction about the tale they were to tell there. To the people of Lewis they were to explain that old Mr. Sinclair, his son, and Mr. Graham were the captain, mate, and bo'sun of a ship wrecked on the Isle of Tiree. They were natives of Orkney, and anxious to return there. In South Uist Clanranald's brother, MacDonald of Boisdale, had given them passage in a boat bound for Stornoway—the eight-oared boat, that is—and in Stornoway they would try to charter a ship that could take them home. They would, moreover—to give some look of realism to the business—declare their intention of buying in Orkney a cargo of meal to send back for sale in Lewis. Old Donald MacLeod, who had formerly engaged in that trade, would be their pilot.

The initial voyage was again stormy, with a strong wind from the south-west, and on the morning of the 29th they went ashore on the island of Scalpay near the mouth of Loch Seaforth, a long and narrow fjord that runs far into the Lewis. The tenant of Scalpay was Donald Campbell, who, as it appears, had so mitigated the Whiggery of his family as to marry a MacDonald woman described as 'a rigid loyalist'. Campbell of Scalpay proved a true friend to the Prince, and his first remembered benefaction was to light a good fire; for the travellers were cold. For one night Donald MacLeod stayed in Scalpay, and the next morning—leaving the others under Campbell's hospitable roof—sailed for Stornoway in a borrowed boat.

There he succeeded in chartering a brig of forty tons for the sum of £100 sterling; or so says Captain Alexander MacDonald in his narrative, though Donald MacLeod, in his account, makes no mention of an actual bargain. MacDonald goes on to explain that the master of the brig then grew suspicious, went back on his word, and refused to contemplate a charter at any price. A rumour, it is obvious, had reached Stornoway that Charles was somewhere in the Long Island; and perhaps Donald himself, that valiant old seaman, was indiscreet. He was certainly less than prudent—if Captain MacDonald's story is trustworthy—when he offered to buy the brig for £300, and then agreed to the captain's demand for £500. Such extravagance could only be explained by the supposition that he was acting for the Prince. That being so, the captain made it clear that he himself would not sail in the brig, even if Donald could find his promised £500, but said his mate and the crew would go. They, however, refused to sail unless their own captain was in command; and the whole plan seemed doomed to failure.

One of the first to have heard of the Prince's arrival in the Long Island was the Rev. John Macaulay, minister of South Uist, whose grandson, the historian Lord Macaulay, would in the course of time captivate parliament and charm a multitude of readers with the delusive brilliance of his gifts. The Rev. John's father was Aulay Macaulay, minister of Harris: 'a devil of a minister who did us a' the mischief in his power,' according to one Duncan Cameron, sometime a servant of Lochiel. It was he who sent word, through another minister, to the people of Stornoway that a dangerous visitor had come to the island; and Donald MacLeod's quest for a ship would give substance to the report.

A sense of duty was not the Rev. Aulay's only motive. There was a price of £30,000 on the Prince's head, and with an unnamed neighbour the minister of Harris organised a small, armed invasion of Scalpay in the hope of capturing so valuable a fugitive. They were defeated by the intransigent good faith of Donald Campbell who, though no Jacobite, respected the old laws of hospitality and had no appetite for blood-money. He stood stoutly against the boat-load of armed men who

*Highlander with pipes that were*
*played at Culloden*

came to his island, gave his guests time to make ready for defence, and warned the invaders that they would have to fight for their prize. At that their hearts failed them—or the Rev. Aulay may have deprecated bloodshed—and the fortune-hunters, shame-faced and disappointed, returned to Harris. In the five months of the Prince's wandering this was the only attempt to take advantage of the bribe that the Hanoverian government offered; though in the 18th century £30,000 was a vast sum of money.

In Stornoway Donald refused to recognise the failure of his mission, and it must be that he still expected to take delivery of the brig, though without captain or crew. His own crew, of the eight-oared boat, were now in Stornoway, and they could sail a ship of that size. He sent a messenger to the Prince at Scalpay to say he had found a suitable vessel, and the Prince, with O'Sullivan, O'Neil, and a guide went over to Harris and set out on a long walk. They rowed, to begin with, up the long, bent arm of Loch Seaforth, and landed in wild country near the head of it. Harris, which is the southern quarter of the island of Lewis, consists largely of water and hill. The hills are desolate and high—a grim cluster of naked heights as tall as 2,500 feet—and many small lochs lie in open moorland surrounded by soft, black bogs. It was by night that Charles and his party started to walk from the top of Loch Seaforth to Stornoway: a night when there would be no moon till half-past two.

Their guide lost his way, in wet and stormy weather, and one account says they walked thirty-eight miles before coming in sight of the town; another, which seems to substantiate it, that they were eighteen hours on the hill. The guide was sent on, to find Donald and bring back a bottle of brandy and some bread and cheese; for as Donald himself reports, with a fine simplicity, 'they stood much in need of a little refreshment.'

Donald, with brandy and bread, came promptly to their aid, and took them to the house of Kildun in Arnish, a couple of miles from Stornoway, where 'Lady Kildun', a Mrs. Mackenzie, befriended them.

40

*The empty croft*

She put whisky and eggs and milk on the table, and made up a roaring fire. The Prince put off his shirt, and someone took it to the door to wring it half-dry; then spread it on a chair before the fire. Donald, still confident that the brig would be available, went back to Stornoway. There he was astonished to find two or three hundred men in arms, whose leaders received him very angrily and accused him of having exposed them to grave danger. They were now convinced, not only that the Prince was in their neighbourhood, but that he commanded an army five hundred strong: such, they said, was the story sent by the Rev. John Macaulay to his father the Rev. Aulay, and by him to Mr. Colin Mackenzie, a Presbyterian preacher in the Lewis.

Donald, according to his own story, expostulated hotly, told them that the Prince had only two companions, 'and when I am there I make the third.' Then, if his memory can be trusted—and a little embellishment would not much discredit him—he added indignantly, 'And yet let me tell you farther, gentlemen, if Seaforth himself were here, by God he durst not put a hand to the Prince's breast.'

Most of Lewis was Mackenzie country, and the Earl of Seaforth, the Mackenzie chief, had preferred the rational arguments of Duncan Forbes of Culloden to Jacobite adventure; but the sentiment of his clan was mixed. Donald stresses the fact that among the angry men of Stornoway there was no animosity to the Prince himself, no intention of doing him the smallest hurt; but devoutly they wished to get rid of him, and would do nothing to help him. Donald, it seems, was still keeping an eye on the brig, though two of the crew of the eight-oared boat, frightened by so many armed men, had now run away; but that part of the mainland shore on which it was hoped to land the Prince was unknown to him, and the Stornoway men refused absolutely to let him have a pilot. Donald had to return to Kildun House and admit defeat.

Exhausted by his long walk, the Prince refused to move until he had had a few hours' sleep. He and O'Sullivan and O'Neil had six shirts between them, but their spare shirts were as wet as those they had worn, and they were still hungry. They killed one of Mrs. Mackenzie's cows, and found her unwilling to take payment for it. When she did accept the money, she gave them a present of butter and bread, and they left Kildun with parcels of cow-beef, two pecks of meal, plenty of brandy and sugar, and a wooden platter on which to make dough. A good boat belonging to Donald Campbell lay not far away, and on the morning of the 6th May they embarked with the six remaining men of their original crew—Ned Burke and old Donald's son were still with them—and put to sea with the intention of returning to Scalpay. But now the English frigates had returned from St. Kilda, and some were cruising off-shore. So to avoid them they put in to the small desert island of Iubhard at the mouth of Loch Shell, some twelve miles from Stornoway, having to beat against a strong, contrary wind.

There, for four days and nights, they sheltered in a wretched hut, but found more sustenance than might have been expected. The Lewis fishermen used Iubhard to dry or wind-cure their cod and haddock, and the fugitives had all the dried fish they wanted, and an earthen pitcher in which, with their brandy and sugar and spring-water, they could brew warm punch; until, on their second night, someone broke the pitcher. Occasionally, it is said, the Prince would drink a toast to a black-eyed princess of France, and protest his great trust in the French king; though he would add, as a warning against too much hope, that 'a King and his Council are two very different things.' He was a genial and helpful companion in that miserable, almost roofless hut on the desolate islet, and shared the cooking with Ned Burke. He is given particular credit, indeed, for baking a bannock made of meal and the brains of Mrs. Mackenzie's cow. But he and 'the gentlemen' ate apart from the boatmen, whose table was only a big stone on the bare ground.

On the 10th May it was thought safe to continue their voyage, and the Prince insisted on their going first to Scalpay, to let him pay his respects to Donald Campbell and arrange for the hire of his good boat;

43

but Campbell was no longer there. He had had to go into hiding to escape reprisal for the help he had given to Charles; or to avoid the hostility of the Rev. Aulay Macaulay. On Scalpay, indeed, they were alarmed by the approach of four strangers, and returned to their boat in a hurry.

They rowed and sailed south along the coast towards Benbecula, and hunger persuaded them to make a poor meal of salt-water *drammach*: oatmeal stirred to a paste with sea-water, that is. But they still had a bottle or two of spirits, and a dram all round improved its flavour. Then off Finsbay in Harris they were alarmed by a man-of-war, H.M.S. *Furness*, Captain Ferguson, who promptly gave chase under full sail. They too carried sail, and putting out their oars to increase their speed steered into shoal water near Rodel Point, and drew away from their pursuer. Ferguson made another attempt to head them off, but now the tide was ebbing and the little boat with its shallow draught could sail close to the dangerous islets in the Sound of Harris. Ferguson turned away, and old Donald steered to Lochmaddy; but there another frigate lay. Again they took to the oars, and after a night at sea, off the broken shore of North Uist, they reached a little island in Loch Uskavagh in Benbecula. Scarcely had they landed when the wind blew up to a strong gale, with heavy rain, and they took shelter in what is described as 'a poor grass-keeper's hut or bothy', the door of which was so low that the boatmen dug below it to let the Prince enter more comfortably. There they stayed for three nights, presumably till the weather improved, and fed well enough on sea-birds and fish.

From Uskavagh the Prince and some others landed in Benbecula, where they called at the house of old Clanranald. He advised them of a good refuge, so they continued across country to Corradale in South Uist, where a rough inlet in the rocky coast is overlooked by Hekla to the north and Ben More to the south, each of them about 2,000 feet in height. A cave in a little landward cliff is the Prince's traditional hiding-place, but here tradition has gone astray; for there is no word of a cave

44

*Hold fast*

in contemporary accounts. Donald MacLeod describes the refuge as 'a tenant's house, only a hut better than ordinary'; and it has been called a forester's cottage. There, in tolerable comfort and relative safety, Charles stayed for three weeks; and his immunity can rouse no surprise in anyone who has seen Corradale. No road approaches it from any side, there are no signs of nearby habitation, and from the sea there is no access save by a rough scramble over weed-hung rocks. Hekla on the one side, Ben More on the other, stand like guardians of its secrecy, and often between them hangs a cloud-curtain of forbidding grey. Who formerly lived in the cottage that sheltered the Prince is not known; despite its alleged superiority to others of the same sort, it may have been built—not for regular tenancy or a forester—but for cow-herds when the cattle were turned out to summer pasture.

The King's ships were patrolling the Minches: *Greyhound*, *Baltimore*, and *Terror*, the sloop of war *Raven* and the *Furness*, H.M.SS. *Scarborough* and *Glasgow*, the sloops *Trial* and *Happy Janet*; but from the sea the Prince's cottage was invisible. To a good many people in South Uist his presence was known, but they, even if not committed to the Jacobite cause, were well-disposed and trustworthy. All, that is, except one; of whom Ned Burke told the following story.

The Prince, walking one day with a musket on his shoulder, saw a running deer—fired offhand—and killed it. (He is said, elsewhere, to have been a very good shot.) Ned Burke, who was with him or near at hand, brought in the deer—the little island stags are not heavy—and having done his butcher's job, was cutting some collops when a poor vagrant boy came up and lovingly began to finger the fresh meat. Burke gave him 'a whip with the back of his hand', and was promptly reproved by the Prince, who, says Burke, spoke to him of 'Scripture which reminds us to feed the hungry and cleed the naked.'

'You ought rather to give him meat than a stripe,' said the Prince, and added, 'I cannot see a Christian perish for want of food and raiment had I the power to support them.' That Burke elaborates, and builds a

46

*A croft in South Uist*

pious tale on a kindly gesture, is not to be doubted—he goes so far as to picture the Prince, now taking full advantage of the situation, uttering an extempore prayer for 'the poor and needy'—but though Burke fails to command our full belief, his memory of the Prince's compassion for a shivering and hungry boy is an agreeable and perfectly credible addition to the legend. Charles's religion was not unduly dogmatic or portentously apparent, but elsewhere—much later in the story—there is sound testimony to the fact that every morning he would go apart to say his prayers.

Burke's conclusion to the tale is that the boy, having been fed and clothed, ran off, 'like Judas', and betrayed his benefactor. The pursuit of the Prince, and his pursuers, had now reached the Long Island. Redcoats had landed in Barra, militia-men in Benbecula and the Uists. As the pursuit gathered strength, so the search was intensified; though to begin with it was perfunctory. If Burke can be believed the ungrateful boy got only ridicule for his story that the Prince was in Corradale, and was told that he deserved to be thrown into the sea for talking such pernicious nonsense. If that is true, the explanation must be that some, at least, of the militia-men and their officers, though nominally in the Hanoverian service, had in fact no urgent wish to deliver Charles to Hanoverian justice.

The account of his sojourn in Corradale has indeed a roughly idyllic quality. He had there a fairly numerous retinue. O'Sullivan, O'Neil, Father Allan MacDonald, and several other MacDonalds were with him, and enough of the humbler sort to provide a kind of bodyguard. Visitors came to enliven the cottage with their conversation, and Clanranald brought the welcome present of a few clean shirts, some stockings, and a pair of shoes; as well as wine and brandy. He came again, it seems, and brought a suit of clothes, a tartan suit that greatly pleased the Prince. 'I only want the itch,' he said, 'to be a complete highlander.'

He had, for a throne, a seat of turf softened by moss and a folded plaid, and in the cottage was a lesser room that served as a pantry; and

*An island crofter*

there, when he felt the need of a dram, he would put a bottle of whisky or brandy to his lips and drink without ceremony. He had a hard head for drink, and there is a story of a great carousal when a party of lively MacDonalds came to Corradale and drank all night. They drank cold brandy out of clean sea-shells, and there was much talk of politics and religion. The Prince declared that there were few of Europe's rulers who had any sense or notion of religion, but his own faith was fairly evident. The end of the drinking-bout was the collapse of all save Charles. Among his guests was MacDonald of Boisdale, respected as one of the best men with a bottle to be found in Scotland; but even he was on the floor before morning. And the Prince, covering his weaker friends with their plaids, sang '*De Profundis*' for the good of their souls.

He took his pleasure out of doors as well, for in those days South Uist was wonderfully rich in game. In Captain Alexander MacDonald's narrative it is written that 'His Royal Highness was pretty oft at his diversion through the mountains, papping down perhaps dozens in a day of muircocks and hens'—grouse, that is, though the month was May —'with which this place abounds; for he is most dextrous at shooting all kinds of fowl upon wing, scarce ever making a miss.'

Old Donald MacLeod praises him not only for his unquenchable high spirits—sometimes he would 'sing them a song to keep up their hearts'—but for his ingenuity, liveliness, and faculty of making the most of small comforts. He was a pipe-smoker, and clay pipes are frail. In his rough way of life his pipes used to break and turn into 'short cutties'; whereupon Charles would lengthen them with the quills of sea-birds' feathers till the stem was long enough to let them smoke coolly. Captain Alexander MacDonald says 'his magnanimous spirit bore all crosses and adversities with the greatest Christian resignation and manly courage'; but Ned Burke, speaking of his relations with Father Allan MacDonald, makes it fairly clear that Charles was not unduly subservient to authority: 'Faith, I have reason to think the Prince is not a great Papist, for he never gree'd well with the priest at all, and was very easy about his

50

company.'—Easy, too, about his comfort, for when Ned was cursing his luck for having lost a shoe, the Prince called, 'Ned, look at me!' And held up a shoe that had lost its sole. 'O my dear,' cried Ned, 'I have nothing more to say. You have stopt my mouth indeed.'

There were times, of course, when Charles admitted depression, and times when he spoke with foolish confidence, or wistfully perhaps, of the power of France and what the French king would do for him. But, in the main, memories coalesce to make the portrait of a remarkably attractive young man: sturdy and resilient, uncommonly equable in face of dire misfortune and fearful discomfort, and delightfully at his ease with the rough honesty of Ned Burke or the oaken worth of Donald MacLeod. He had, moreover, had to learn to accommodate himself to primitive disabilities and the raw life of adventure. Less than a year before he had spent his first night in Scotland on the island of Eriskay—a day or two before the *Doutelle* landed him on the shore of Loch nan Uamh—and there, in a house so well furnished as to have sheets on the bed, he had looked narrowly at the sheets before deciding to sit up all night; and had angered his host by repeatedly going to the door for fresh air. 'What a plague is the matter with that fellow, that he can neither sit nor stand still, and neither keep within nor without doors?' exclaimed Angus MacDonald of Eriskay. There was nothing the matter with the house, nothing at all but for the fire being in the middle of the floor, with no chimney except a hole in the roof, and the room full of smoke. In 1745 Charles had been a little hard to please, but in 1746 it was much more difficult to disconcert him.

While he remained in Corradale old Donald had been sent to the mainland to get what money he could from John Murray of Broughton. Murray had joined the Prince at Kinloch Moidart in August of the previous year, and been appointed his principal secretary a few days later.—It was at this time that Charles first heard of the reward of £30,000 offered for his capture; and proposed, in return a reward of £30 for the person of George II.—Murray was now at Loch Arkaig with Lochiel and some others, and the Prince had good reason to hope for a substantial sum, for on the 3rd May two French frigates, *Bellona* and *Mars*, had landed 40,000 louis d'or with arms and ammunition in Loch nan Uamh.

It was a daring foray that the French ships made, their purpose being not only to bring aid to the Jacobite forces—if any organised force remained—but to rescue those of their leaders who preferred the safety of France to skulking in Highland hills. While at anchor in the loch the Frenchmen were surprised and attacked by H.M.S. *Greyhound*, Captain Howe—later Lord Howe—and the sloops *Baltimore* and *Terror*. A brisk engagement began, and the battle lasted for four hours with considerable loss on either side. No ship was sunk, but after Howe had run in between the French frigates and given each a broadside, one of them was disabled with a damaged rudder and Howe was out of ammunition. The battle was broken off, and with a discreet distance between them the French and British crews set to work to repair their ships. One of the Frenchmen took aboard the ailing Duke of Perth, who died at sea; Lord John Drummond, Lord Elcho, the Prince's old tutor Sir Thomas Sheridan; and at two o'clock in the morning *Bellona* and *Mars* stood out to sea and with a fair wind made for Barra Head.

They deserved good fortune after so hazardous an enterprise. It must be noted, however, that the French captains appear to have landed a valuable cargo without much consideration about who should receive it. It may be that English topsails had been sighted, and they were in a hurry. On the shore of the loch were a leash of young MacDonalds, and the captain of the *Terror* wrote that he had seen them carrying off chests of arms and barrels that, he thought, contained powder. But the barrels may have been more richly filled, for some days later a hostile critic, Campbell of Auchindoun, declared the MacDonalds had stolen £1,000 in money and no less than 240 casks of brandy. Auchindoun was no friend of Clan Donald, and evidently the thought of good French brandy going down their rascally throats had enraged him beyond reason; for all the MacDonalds in Arisaig could hardly have carried off so vast a booty. There may, however, have been some genial drunkenness on the beach, as he suggests; and it was there, perhaps, that the 40,000 louis d'or began to disappear.

Murray of Broughton, though enfeebled and ill, had not fled to France, but remained to do his duty, as well as he could, and see to the proper distribution of the money or its effective concealment. By his instruction it was taken to somewhere in Lochaber, but what finally happened to it has never been properly decided. Government troops searched for it in vain, and some otherwise respectable Scottish gentlemen may have helped themselves to it in passing. Many believed it to have been buried near Loch Arkaig, and for several years there was undignified squabbling about who had seen it, who had had it, and what had been done with it; but finally the 'Loch Arkaig treasure', as it was called, disappeared even from hope of recovery, and the manner of its disappearance became a cherished mystery like the murder in Appin of Colin Campbell of Glenure a few years later.

What emerges positively from the story is that Charles could have saved himself a great deal of discomfort if, instead of sailing to Benbecula, he had stayed in Arisaig and waited for the *Mars* and *Bellona*. Had he done so, however, he would have deprived Scotland of both a legend and a mystery. His own legend would have been incomplete and unsatisfying; and the Loch Arkaig treasure would probably have remained aboard. All Scotland is permanently the richer by his mistake, and in his own lifetime a few Highland chiefs were temporarily enriched.

But Donald MacLeod, seeking replenishment for the Prince's purse, was again disappointed. He met Lochiel and Murray of Broughton, and got no money from them. Justifiably the Prince had a high opinion of Murray, as a firm and honest man, but Murray may have spoken a little disingenuously when he told Donald that all he had was sixty louis d'or, 'which was not worth the while to send.' He and Lochiel gave him letters for the Prince, and Donald found means to buy two ankers of brandy at a guinea an anker; if the Dutch measure was in use this means he got, for a guinea, rather more than eight imperial gallons, and in that transaction was certainly not cheated. He had come from Corradale in Donald Campbell's good boat, and in her, a little more deeply laden, returned to find the Prince and his companions upset by new alarms. Their three weeks of holiday were at an end, and again they must take to the hills and the sea to evade capture.

# VI

CAPTAIN Ferguson of the sloop-of-war *Furness* was reported to have put some hundreds of regular soldiers ashore on Barra. Three hundred MacLeods of Skye, enlisted or conscribed in a local militia, had gone to Benbecula. The squadron whose troops were commanded by General Campbell of Mamore had returned from their vain errand to St. Kilda and disembarked in the Uists. The narrow seas between the Long Island and Skye and the mainland were full of hostile ships, all searching for the Prince. The little period of easy-going, Highland ambivalence was at an end. The hunt was up, and now the hunt became deadly serious.

A couple of trustworthy MacDonalds, nephews of Captain Alexander, were sent north and south to observe and report the movements of Ferguson's redcoats and the MacLeod militia, and came back with the news that both were to search the intervening country till they met in the middle. It was time to leave Corradale, and they still had Campbell of Scalpay's good boat. The Prince and the two Irishmen, O'Sullivan and O'Neil, with Donald MacLeod, Ned Burke, and some others went aboard and sailed north to Ouia—or Wiay, as the maps spell it—a little island off Benbecula. It was now the 5th June. In Ouia they remained for a couple of nights, utterly at a loss, as one imagines, what to do next. Then the Prince and O'Neil, with a guide, went to Rossinish, where they found Lady Clanranald: Rossinish where they had first landed on the 27th April was by sea only some five miles north of Ouia, but to walk there must have meant a longer march than that. And after a couple of nights in Rossinish the only advice the Prince could get was that he had better go back to the island.

How to do this was not clear. The militia-men were combing the hills and using boats to search the shore. But what escapes, again and again, from the narratives—sometimes formal and stiff, sometimes ingenuous—of those who shared Charles's adventure, and lived to tell of it, is that an underground news-service was always maintained. Anonymous men, or gangling boys and girls of seeming innocence, went to and fro between the Prince's company and the houses of his suspect friends—between those houses and the enemy—to warn him of danger in such-and-such a quarter, of a new militia company ordered into new quarters. He had scores of secret well-wishers—hundreds, it may be—who knew enough to win the Government's great reward for his capture, but rather than a fortune of £30,000 chose to succour him and walk stealthily by night to whisper softly in the darkness of a menace beyond the hill or a frigate in the sea-loch to the north. O'Sullivan and Donald MacLeod had stayed in Ouia when Charles and O'Neil went to Rossinish, and having been told of his predicament they put to sea, under cover of night, and again with the help of unknown messengers met him on the shore at Rossinish, and sailed south again towards Corradale. They had heard, presumably, that Corradale had been searched, and now for a little while might be safe again, because the militia-men had left it to look elsewhere.

As so often before, however, they ran into foul weather. June is commonly a mild and sunlit month in the Outer Hebrides, but wherever he went the Prince was likely to meet fugitive's weather: wind and rain, that is, which added to his discomfort but impeded pursuit. Now, on that rocky coast, they met a roaring gale, with rain pouring from the galloping clouds, and were forced to make a rough landing at Ushinish Point, a couple of miles north of Corradale. They found refuge, north again from there, at a desolate corner called, on the map, Acairseil Falaich. It was no better than a cleft in the rock, but for a whole day, while the gale continued, it gave them shelter from the enemy. But not, as it seems, from friendly eyes. For again they were warned that hostile troops were no more than two miles away; and the weather having moderated, they put to sea and headed south to Kyle Stuley, not far from Loch Boisdale.

To trace, at this time, their coastwise voyaging is not unlike mapping the course of a water-beetle; but now their erratic passages, their turning and doubling, were, so far from being aimless, quite certainly dictated by news of the enemy's dispositions. From Corradale north to Ouia,

*Lobster creels*

from Ouia to Rossinish; back towards Corradale but forced by storm on to the rocks of Ushinish; thence to Kyle Stuley, and a venture to Loch Boisdale; a quick turn-about at the sight of three men-of-war, then south again, and no safety in the loch, but up and down its shores; then north, once more, over the hills to Ormaclett.—Between the 5th and 21st June that is a record of the Prince's movement, and never was he far from the fear of capture unless rough seas presented a closer fear.

He had hoped to get help from MacDonald of Boisdale, but on their first approach, in the darkness, they were alarmed by a strange shape at the entrance to the loch that some took for a long-boat full of marines. Donald MacLeod told them it was only a rock, but when three ships were seen within cannon-shot of the shore, prudence sent them back to Kyle Stuley for another night. Again they ventured south, this time by day, and in Loch Boisdale got the ill news that MacDonald had been made prisoner. This was a savage blow, for Boisdale had skilfully maintained a benign neutrality. He had stayed peacefully at home, he had kept most of the island MacDonalds from following their young chief Clanranald, and for the last few weeks had done all he could to shield the Prince from danger. His imprisonment was quite unexpected, and the Prince was much distressed by it. It was Boisdale who had sent the secret messengers who always arrived in time to warn the fugitives of imminent or approaching danger. He knew the safest hiding-places, and because many MacDonalds were officers in the militia he got useful information about troop movements. If Boisdale had remained at liberty, the Prince need never have left the Long Island; or so Donald MacLeod and others believed.

Their approach to the loch had been hindered by a fleet of fifteen sail. Before they could enter, the Prince and his companions had had to pull their boat into a narrow creek, seemingly behind the islet of Calvey on the south shore, and wait for dusk. They went that night to an old tower on Calvey, where they lighted a fire and cooked some food while Ned Burke was pulling heather for the Prince's bed. But

*The ruins of Calvey Castle, near*
*Loch Boisdale*

a new alarm prevented sleep. Two more ships were sighted, which Donald MacLeod thought were French. But when they came nearer they were seen to be English, and the Prince, with three others, took to the hills, while the rest of his party rowed higher up the loch.

The men-of-war did not enter the loch, and later that night the fugitives were re-united on the shore; there was still some food in the boat, though not much. It is not known exactly when they first heard of Boisdale's imprisonment, but they were not without means of communication, for Lady Boisdale sent them four bottles of brandy and other comforts. For a couple of nights they lay on the open hillside, sheltered only by the sails of the boat. Then they went farther up the loch, and found a hiding-place where they remained for two nights more. They were warned of the approach of redcoats and a Campbell militia company, and crossed over to the north side. A Captain Caroline Scott, of evil reputation, landed within a mile of them, and again the party separated; the Prince, with O'Neil and a guide, took to the hills.

Before he left the others Charles told O'Sullivan to pay the boatmen their wages, of a shilling a day, and to Donald MacLeod he gave an order on John Hay of Restalrig for sixty pistoles—about £50—'if he should happen to be so lucky as to meet with him upon the continent.' (The mainland of Scotland, that is.) It was a woeful parting between the Prince and Donald, and years later the old man would still weep to tell of it. They spoke of a rendezvous, but neither can have had much hope of meeting again. Now it was *sauve qui peut*, and only one of the boatmen stayed with Donald. They sank the boat—Campbell of Scalpay's good boat, that had served them so well—and despite the redcoats and militia who scoured the island, found their way to Benbecula again. There, on the 5th July, Donald was made prisoner, and what happened to him must be told before continuing the tale of the Prince's flight.

From Benbecula he and other prisoners were taken to Barra, then to Skye; where, to Donald's mortification, some of his own relations refused to speak to him. From Skye he went over to Applecross, and was put aboard Captain Ferguson's ship *Furness,* to be taken before General Campbell. Their conversation was later recorded by Donald himself.

When the General asked if he had been with the young Pretender, he answered, 'Yes, I was along with that young gentleman, and I winna deny it.'

'Do you know,' said the General, 'what money was upon that man's head? £30,000 sterling, which would have made you and all your children after you happy for ever.'

'What then?' said Donald. '£30,000! Though I had gotten't I could not have enjoyed it eight and forty hours. Conscience would have gotten up upon me. That money could not have kept it down. And tho' I could have gotten all England and Scotland for my pains I would not allowed a hair of his body to be touch'd if I could help it.'

To which the General replied, 'I will not say that you are in the wrong.'—Donald insisted, to do Campbell justice, that these were his very words.

More interrogation followed, and when the General heard that a priest had sailed with them through the great storm in the eight-oared boat, he asked if he had busied himself with prayers for the young Pretender's safety.

'Na, good faith he, Sir,' said Donald, 'for if he prayed for himsell, he thought he did well enough. And had you been there, Sir, you would have thought you did well enough too if you had prayed for yoursell. Every one of us was minding himsell then.'

The General was a man of agreeable temper, but on the evidence of Donald and many others Captain Ferguson's behaviour was habitually barbarous. Prisoners aboard his ship lived in wretched conditions; and Donald and those with him were confined aboard, without trial, till April of the following year. Then at Tilbury they were transferred to a prison-hulk where they lay in extreme misery, still without trial. He was finally given his liberty on the 10th June, 1747.

# VII

WHEN the Prince and O'Neil left the others on the shore of Loch Boisdale, and headed north across the moor, their guide was Neil MacEachain, who had presumably been sent to their help by Lady Clanranald; for MacEachain, a schoolmaster in South Uist, was also tutor in Clanranald's family; he was at dinner with Clanranald and the Rev. John Macaulay when news arrived that the Prince had landed in Benbecula. He was a clever young man who had gone to the Scots College in Paris to study for the church, but had changed his mind and come home again. He spoke French, which was a comfort to Charles, and was very good-natured. He was, however, said to be timorous, and there were those who doubted his capacity for service of a sort that was bound to be dangerous and demanded absolute fidelity. He was, it seems, a small man of no particular presence, and those who mistook him for a servant of Flora MacDonald's had the excuse, perhaps, that he always behaved with a pleasant modesty. In the event he became one of Charles's most reliable adherents.

Fionnghal MacDonald, anglified as Flora, who appears 'in the nick of time'—the phrase is entirely appropriate, for the story is now of hurried and desperate adventure—was the daughter of Ranald Mac-Donald of Milton in South Uist, of the family of Clanranald, and of Marion MacDonald from Griminish in North Uist. Her father died when Flora was two years old, and her mother married yet another MacDonald, Hugh of Armadale in Skye. Flora, who in 1746 was twenty-four, had a younger brother, Angus, who had succeeded to Milton when he came of age, and Flora—though she and her step-father were on the friendliest terms—went to keep house for him. But she may have been staying with Clanranald when he learnt of the Prince's arrival at Rossinish, and assuredly she had heard every tale or rumour of him since that stormy day. More than once, indeed, she had met O'Neil, who before the man-hunt grew so fierce and urgent had become friendly with her brother Angus, and visited the house of Milton.

The ambivalent attitude of the MacDonald officers in the local militia has already been noted—Boisdale could rely on them for news of troop movements—and according to MacEachain, who like several others wrote a narrative of the great adventure, it was none other than Captain Hugh MacDonald, Flora's stepfather, who proposed the means by which at last Charles made his escape from the Long Island. Lady Clanranald was privy to the plot, but Flora herself was unaware of her stepfather's connivance.

It was the night of the 21st June—the short darkness was lighted by a full moon—when the Prince and O'Neil, led by MacEachain, walked over the moor to Ormaclett on the west side of South Uist, about three miles from Milton. The house of Ormaclett, which belonged to an older Clanranald, had been burnt thirty years before, on the day when that Clanranald fell at Sheriffmuir, but nearby was a summer shieling where Flora had gone to tend her brother's cattle. MacEachain must have known where to find her, but O'Neil claims that it was 'by good fortune' they met. It is fairly clear that O'Neil was much attracted to Flora, and wholly clear that he was jealous of MacEachain; jealous, perhaps, of MacEachain's familiar acquaintance with Flora, and certainly jealous of her preference for MacEachain when they put to sea and sailed to Skye; for O'Neil, in the journal that he wrote, never mentions the name of Neil MacEachain.

O'Neil's story, which is true enough but for that omission, is that he approached the shieling to ask if Flora expected any militia-men to be passing on the following day. Not that day but the next, she said; for the heather-line still transmitted news. O'Neil said he had brought a friend to see her, and Flora, showing a natural emotion—she may have felt as much fear as warmth of loyalty—asked if it was the Prince. It was, said O'Neil, and went a little way apart to where Charles was waiting, and led him to the low door of the shieling. He saluted her kindly, and Flora set a dish of cream on the table.

They spoke of the Prince's imminent danger, and O'Neil suggested that the safest and likeliest way of procuring his escape was for her to 'convey him'—that is the phrase he uses—to the Isle of Skye, where her mother lived. It would be easy for her to do that, he said, because her stepfather, an officer in the militia, could give her a passport for herself and a servant. Charles agreed with what O'Neil had said, and asked Flora if she would help him. Flora answered 'with the greatest respect and loyalty', but declined.

It was her belief that O'Neil had contrived the plan, and though she had no reason to doubt his fidelity, she may have distrusted his sagacity. Her excuse, however, was that her stepfather was a captain in a regiment of militia commanded by Sir Alexander MacDonald, one of the two great lairds in Skye, with whom and his wife she was on friendly terms; and her participation in the plot, if it became known, might be Sir Alexander's ruin.

O'Neil argued that Sir Alexander was not, at that time, in Skye— he was in Fort Augustus with Cumberland—and there was no reason to think that he could be accused of connivance. Flora's mother, he said, lived near the shore, and the Prince could be carried to her house without difficulty. Then, he says, he spoke of the honour and immortality she would earn by so glorious an action; and if he did, in fact, speak in such a way, one can be sure that his words had no effect whatever, for Flora was modest, sensible, and serious. It was Charles himself who persuaded her—against her will as she herself says—to undertake a perilous mission whose peril the Irishman had so disingenuously played down. She listened to the Prince's appeal, and acquiesced after he had told her—in O'Neil's florid transcription of his words—of 'the sense he would always retain of so conspicuous a service.'

That was not the sort of language he used to others, and it is unlikely that he addressed his last plea to Flora with such pomposity. It is more probable by far that he cloaked his seriousness in some levity, and appealed, not only to her loyalty, but to the nascent spirit of adventure that her grave and lovely eyes so foolishly betrayed. She was indeed a serious and well-behaved young woman, but then, as it did later in her life, a prospect of danger may have warmed her mind.

If O'Neil, as is possible, threw in a proposal of marriage as her reward, it failed to influence her; but she agreed to make enquiry about the feasibility of the project, and the Prince and his two companions left the little shieling, bathed in the light of a full moon, to march again, now towards the slopes of Hekla, the hill that overlooks the loneliness of Corradale, which three weeks earlier had been holiday-ground.

Flora set out for the Clanranald house of Nunton, on the Atlantic shore of Benbecula, and though no record remains of how she hoped to get there, the inference is plain that while there was urgent, emotional conversation in the moonlit shieling, a couple of her clansmen lay discreetly in the heather, with a pony tethered not far away. She rode towards Nunton with an escort enough for her safety, but insufficiently aware of the nearest militia-men. She was stopped at the ford between South Uist and Benbecula, and the message she had promised to send to the Prince did not arrive.

Charles grew anxious. From where he lay, under a rock on Hekla, he could look across the shining, water-patched lowlands of South Uist to the Benbecula ford, and by afternoon of the next day the view was still empty, and his empty stomach was uncomfortable. MacEachain went off to buy food, and later in the evening the impatient Prince despatched him to find Flora, discover what had happened to her, and what was to be done. At the ford MacEachain was arrested too.

On the Benbecula side, however, MacDonald of Armadale had arrived, and by morning was in command of the situation. Neither of his prisoners was detained for long. Flora, his stepdaughter, was able to tell MacEachain that she would go, as she had intended, to Nunton; make due preparation there; and wait for the Prince at Rossinish. As soon as MacEachain was released, he hurried back to the gaunt slope of Hekla and saw Charles sitting under the great rock where he had left him. The Prince ran to meet him, and demanded his news.

65

Now they faced the difficulty of getting to Rossinish: the physical and nervous difficulty of moving through closely guarded country, under a head-burden of £30,000, to a shore that might be patrolled by watchful marines. There was a small boat fishing in Loch Skiport whose crew were persuaded to take them to the familiar desolation of Ouia; but there was no one on Ouia to help them—no one there at all—and the fishermen rowed them across to the nearest point of Benbecula. They hoped to find their way through that tormented landscape of bogs and lochs to Rossinish, but the Prince and O'Neil were exhausted. They lay down on the rocks and fell asleep, while MacEachain, the little schoolmaster, kept watch.

They had been put ashore, as it happened, on a tidal island, and as MacEachain walked here and there, he observed, in his own words, 'an arm of the sea come in betwixt him and the rest of the land, which formed an island; he returned immediately and informed the Prince, who started up like a madman and walked to the end of the island at such a rate as if he had a mind to fly over to the other side, but his career was soon stopped; whereupon he fell a scoulding MacEachain as if it had been his fault, and the cursed rascals (meaning the boatmen) who landed them upon that desert island designedly that he might starve with hunger and cold, in short, there was no pacifying him, till, at last, MacEachain told him to comfort himself, that he would sweem over to the other side and would bring a boat in half an hour's time. From that time he never gave MacEachain one minutes's rest, till, to please him, he began to strip, notwithstanding that it rained most prodigiously.'—It was lucky for the schoolmaster that the tide then began visibly to ebb.

It is the very same situation as Robert Louis Stevenson contrived for his hapless hero David Balfour in *Kidnapped*, and the Prince's predicament in a later period of his wanderings may have suggested to Stevenson a subsequent passage in the novel. For both the Prince and David Balfour their immediate problem was solved when the ebbing tide left them a dry crossing; but before Charles and O'Neil lay the watery desert of Benbecula's east coast, a land fretted and broken by the invading sea, riddled with lochans, sodden with drenched and sable peat-bog; and heavy rain lashed their faces with the weight of the north-west wind behind it. At last, about midnight, they came to the cottage where Lady Clanranald and Flora were to meet them; but instead of finding the ladies, they got the startling news that a company of militia-men were in camp a few hundred yards away.

Again the Prince lost control of himself, stormed and raged, 'not knowing where to run for safety,' says MacEachain, 'the enemy being everywhere.' A cow-herd who lodged in the cottage took them to a bothy a mile or two away, and when the Prince had recovered his composure he told O'Neil that he must go to Nunton and learn what had happened to Flora and Lady Clanranald. The Irishman was certainly in love, for in his own narrative he makes no mention of the hardship of setting out again, on that abominable night, after their agonising march, but merely reports that Flora told him 'she had engaged a cousin of hers in North Uist to receive him'—the Prince, that is—'in his house, where she was sure he would be more safe than in the Isle of Skye.'

While O'Neil was walking to Nunton, the Prince and MacEachain had been warned by the cow-herd's wife to find a hiding-place on the shore, for the militia-men came to the bothy in the morning to get milk. The rain came down, heavy and remorseless, and the Prince endured it under a rock that gave him no shelter whatever. Now the wind had fallen, the air was mild, and the Hebridean midges came out in swarms. Such was their torment that once more his composure gave way, and in sheer physical despair he sat, wet through, and uttered 'hideous cries and complaints.'

The cow-herd's child kept watch, and after three interminable hours brought word that the militia-men had gone. The Prince returned to the bothy, and presently, in nothing but his shirt, sat warming himself before a great peat-fire. Resilient as ever, his spirits revived, he grew merry and wanted to know if there was anything to eat. 'Nothing,' said the cow-herd's wife, 'except a chapin of milk she kept for her bairns.' MacEachain told her to bring it to the boil and beat it to a froth. She put the pot before them, and gave them two roughly made horn spoons. 'What is it?' asked the Prince, and the little schoolmaster had the audacity to play a trick on him. 'Fresh cream,' he said, and the Prince, dipping deep into the scalded milk, burnt his hand and dropped his spoon in the pot. He fell into a great rage, damned the woman for a vile witch—'For she contrived it a purpose that we might burn ourselves!'—but when MacEachain said she should be beaten, and picked up an oar to belabour her, he quickly turned serious and begged him not to touch her.

Under a torn sail, and wrapped in his plaid, he slept on the floor, and in the afternoon a messenger from Nunton brought two bottles of wine and a dressed fowl. He brought, too, news of Flora's suggestion that Charles should go, not to Skye, but to her cousin's house in North Uist. That plan, however, came to nothing, and Skye was again the objective.

The militia, by this time, had left Benbecula, and the Prince sent word to O'Neil to return immediately. But O'Neil, at Nunton, was more comfortable than in the bothy, and more pleasantly engaged. It had been decided to disguise Charles as a woman, so that he could attend Flora as her maid, and she and Lady Clanranald were 'busie night and day' making his dress. It would be better, said O'Neil, for him to wait until all was ready, and then escort the ladies direct to Rossinish. Again the Prince grew impatient—set out too early to go to Rossinish, sat on a hill to watch for Flora, but no one came—and he had to return to the bothy for yet another night.

In the morning—it was the 22nd June—two young MacDonalds, both officers in the militia, came to tell him that a boat had been found and made ready, and they were to be two of his crew.—A pleasanter example of Highland ambivalence could hardly be wished for.—But now, when apparently the stage was clear, and all preparation made for a quiet, untroubled exit, the wings were again filling with his enemies, and the last scene was to be played in a mood of almost intolerable tension against a background of imminent menace.

On that day, when Benbecula was rid of the militia, movement was unimpeded. MacEachain went over to Nunton to escort the ladies, and with Lady Clanranald and her daughter, with Flora and her brother Angus and O'Neil, came back by boat round the north shore of Benbecula to Rossinish. There, in the bothy that had sheltered him when he first set foot on the Long Island, Charles and the young MacDonalds were cooking dinner, and presently the whole party sat down to the spit-roasted 'heart, liver, kidneys etc., of a bullock or sheep.'—In later days Flora remembered what she had eaten, but the manner of the cooking may have left little difference between ox-kidneys and lamb-kidneys.—On the Prince's left sat Lady Clanranald, Flora on his right, and it is not unreasonable to suppose that in the smoky air of the bothy there was a notable relaxation, and jollity as well.

But their meal was interrupted by a sudden, alarming report that General Campbell had landed not far from Nunton with a force of 1,500 men. At that, it seems, they removed in a hurry to somewhere else on the shore of Loch Uskavagh, and in another bothy waited for the return of a fleet-footed scout or spy—more than one, perhaps—who had been sent to gather the latest news. That, when they heard it, was more disconcerting still. Captain Ferguson, with an advance party of General Campbell's force, was already at Nunton, having arrived soon after Lady Clanranald left—he had slept in her bed—and the abominable Captain Caroline Scott was approaching with another large company. According to O'Neil, the Government forces amounted in all to 2,300 men.

Lady Clanranald and her daughter took leave of the Prince, and went home at once. Her house was in danger, and she was needed there: a good many domestic roofs had gone up in flame after soldiers came to call. She found both Ferguson and General Campbell waiting for her, and when Ferguson asked where she had been, she told him that she had been visiting a sick child. General Campbell, in his more genial fashion, said that he proposed to dine with her, but as a preliminary he would like to know the name of the child. Lady Clanranald did not hesitate to supply a name, and said it was now much better. Ferguson declared her story a mere pretence to cover the real purpose of her journey, but the General's presence saved her further embarrassment. Not long afterwards, however, both she and Clanranald were arrested.

In the bothy at Loch Uskavagh there was a painful scene when it became evident that O'Neil must be left behind. Flora's passport, that her stepfather had given her, named a man servant as well as a maid, and MacEachain was the obvious choice, for O'Neil knew no Gaelic. The Prince pleaded with Flora to let him go with them, but Flora, on whose shoulders now lay responsibility for the success of their plan, refused absolutely to take him. Then, with an emotional flourish, Charles declared that he would not embark unless O'Neil came with him. To which O'Neil replied that if there was any demurring of that sort, he would instantly go off on his own, 'being extremely indifferent what became of myself so that his person was safe.' It was a braggart statement but proper to a romantic occasion, and the Irishman, who had given exemplary service to the Prince, cannot be accused, with any severity, of dramatising his predicament.

In the event he found his way through the militia screen and past the redcoats on the shore to South Uist, where he rejoined O'Sullivan; and some days later they made contact with 'a French cutter, commanded by one Dumont.' By common consent O'Sullivan, who was worn out by strain and fatigue, went aboard the cutter, and arrangement was made for a rendezvous at Raasay, where O'Neil hoped to meet the Prince again. Why he too did not take passage with the Frenchman is obscure, but in some unexplained fashion he made his own way to Raasay, only to learn the Prince had left. Nor could he be found in

Skye. O'Neil then crossed to North Uist, where O'Sullivan in the French cutter had promised to meet him should they fail to find each other in Raasay. The cutter did not come, O'Neil was made prisoner, and taken before the brutal Captain Ferguson. He was stripped, and would have been flogged had not an officer of the Scots Fusiliers, then aboard the *Furness*, objected with drawn sword. O'Neil was later taken to Edinburgh Castle.

In a letter that MacDonald of Armadale wrote to his wife, and that Flora carried with her passport, he referred to her maid as 'one Betty Burke, an Irish girl, who, she tells me, is a good spinster.' Who suggested the name is not known, but it was probably O'Neil, with a memory in his mind of Ned Burke the chair-man. The Prince had now to be clothed in his new character, and in the 'Journal taken from the mouth of Miss Flora MacDonald by Dr. Burton of York, when in Edinburgh,' it is reported that 'when all were gone who were not to accompany the Prince in his voyage to the Isle of Skye,' Flora demurely 'desired him to dress himself in his new attire, which was soon done.'

'The company being gone,' says MacEachain, 'the Prince, stript of his own cloathes'—but he still wore breeches and a waistcoat—'was dressed by Miss Flora in his new attire, but could not keep his hands from adjusting his headdress, which he cursed a thousand times. The gown was of calico, a light coloured quilted petticoat, a mantle of dull camlet made after the Irish fashion, with a cap to cover His Royal Highness's whole head and face, with a suitable headdress, shoes, stockings, etc.'

Under his petticoat Charles wanted to wear a pistol, but Flora objected. If he were to be searched, she said, the discovery of a pistol would give him away. To which he answered, 'Indeed, Miss, if we shall happen with any that will go so narrowly to work in searching me as what you mean, they will certainly discover me at any rate.'

In her conversation with Dr. Burton of York, Flora omitted this indelicate joke, but on the authority of Sir Compton Mackenzie—

that devoted Jacobite of our own time—it became, in later years, one of her favourite stories; and deservedly so. That Charles could be dressed-up as Betty Burke, and make a joke of any sort while his embittered enemies were closing in on him, throws a light of agreeable gaiety on his spirit; and to realise that Flora's Highland gravity could be undone by simple laughter warms one's heart almost as much as her heroism. In appearance she was gently severe. Her beauty was not the soft, cosseted kind, but drawn on good bone with the tautness of a clear Hebridean sky, and in her eyes was the profundity that admits, like so much Gaelic song, the inseparable grief of life. It is pleasant to know that her laughter could play comfortably on a little coarseness.

The boat that had been brought to Loch Uskavagh was 'a small shallop of about nine cubits, wright measure'—something less than eighteen feet, presumably—and those who went aboard were Flora, 'Betty Burke', Neil MacEachain, the two MacDonalds on unofficial leave from their militia regiment, Duncan Campbell, and a man whom Flora calls Macmerry; all the crew being natives of the Long Island. They had to wait, on a rainy evening, till the sky darkened, and to warm themselves lighted a fire on the rocky shore. A final alarm drove them into the heather—but not before putting out the fire—when four wherries, with armed men aboard, came into the loch. The enemy passed by without stopping to search the shore, and when the summer dark obscured the sky they put to sea.

There was no wind, and for some hours they had to row. Then, about midnight, it blew hard from the west, with rain in the wind, and the sea rose roughly. But Charles was in high spirits, and sang loudly—'to entertain the company,' said Flora.

She herself, worn out by strain and excitement, fell asleep and lay on the bottom boards where, as she gracefully remembered, 'the Prince carefully guarded her, lest in the darkness any of the men should chance to step upon her.' Once, at some lively movement in the boat, she woke and found him bending over her, warding off with his hands one

*Wings*

of the crew who was moving about to trim the sail. The weather was improving, the wind went down, but now a morning mist lay on the calm sea. They had no compass, and for some little while no knowledge of where they were. But gradually the mist rose, and the coast of Skye showed against a clear morning. That pattern of changeable weather— calm, a rough wind quickly passing, then calm again—gave them fresh trouble, for as they approached the point of the long peninsula of Vaternish, the wind veered to the north-east, blew strongly again, and the crew at the oars could hardly make headway against it. They were exhausted when at last they got into calm water under the lee of the cliffs—'almost ready to breathe out their last,' says MacEachain—and there, in a cleft in the rock-wall, they rested for an hour and ate a hearty but simple meal of bread and butter, drinking water from a rivulet that tumbled over the edge of the cliff. It was Sunday morning, the 19th June.

They pulled round the point of Vaternish, and on the other side of it a pair of sentries shouted at them, and commanded the boat to pull in. One of them ran to call up the guard, the other aimed his piece, but the musket misfired. The crew pulled strongly away, the guard ran down to the shore, and according to one account fired a volley. But MacEachain, the gentle schoolmaster, says not a shot was fired, and the militia-men made no attempt to launch their boat.

They rowed across the broad bay of Loch Snizort to the longer and larger peninsula of Trotternish, and landed where a burn cuts the beach north of Kilbride. It was then about two o'clock in the afternoon.

# VIII

IN the drama, so far described, the weather has played a major part, and there is no disputing the fact that Charles suffered grievous discomfort from cold and violent winds, from heavy rain, and rough seas. It would be a pity, however, if the historically minded traveller of to-day, who wishes to follow his route, were deterred by the Prince's experience. It has been said already that he had fugitive's weather— bad for comfort but good for safety—and in the months of May and June, and even earlier than May, the tourist can expect, with some confidence, a kindlier climate. To substantiate this assertion it may be permissible to speak of the weather in which the film-unit, in May, 1964, photographed some parts of the Prince's route.

In Arisaig and Morar there was brilliant alternation of sun and shower, with long, calm, honey-lighted evenings. The extraordinary contrasts of this part of the country are seen at their best in these conditions. On the tumbled land, much of it precipitous and despite its steepness luxuriantly clad, the dense thickets of rhododendrons flower with an almost tropical brightness—that protruding granite redeems from any association of tropical flabbiness—and the glittering white beaches of Morar shine against a crumbling sea with what looks like a triumphant assertion of the beauty of emptiness. At that time of year they are cold and virginal, imprinted only by the little, arrow footmarks of small wading birds.

The chartered boat, *Western Isles*, that carried the unit to Loch Boisdale, met roughish weather and a lumpy sea, and for some days the southern end of the Long Island was blown upon by strong winds, and lashed occasionally by a pelting rain that was sometimes sharpened by a hail-storm. But no day was wholly unpleasant; there were always rainbow intervals.

Causeways link South Uist and Benbecula, Benbecula and North Uist, so it is possible to drive from Loch Boisdale to Lochmaddy; and most of North Uist is visible from a ring-road. The eastern parts of South Uist and Benbecula are without roads, and can be visited only

*A birch on the beach at Morar*

by those able to walk or charter a boat. Lewis and Harris, the northern part of the Long Island, have an extensive road-system, and it is easy to drive from Stornoway to the head of Loch Seaforth and look, with proper imagination, at the country over which, in darkness, the Prince walked on the night of the 4th May. An indifferent road to Rodel, on the southern corner of Harris, offers views of Scalpay and the broken coast below it. When the *Western Isles*, which had returned to Loch Boisdale, headed east again for Skye, the rain-clouds followed darkness to the west, and a luminous morning broke on a perfectly calm and opalescent sea. The north-western side of Skye is something like a trident with three great prongs of headlands—Dunvegan Head, the Point of Vaternish, and Rudha Hunish, the extremity of Trotternish— and as, one after another, these rose to view, they shaped a misty, grey-and-lemon-tinted landscape that gradually assumed firmer contours and an intricate, fretted aspect. Long bays of an ever deepening blue carried the sea far into a landscape—in that weather—of surprising gentleness, and Loch Snizort was a vast expanse of cerulean calm whose shores, decorated with minute houses and little fields, appeared to be the ultimate refuge of a pastoral people who had never known strife.

It is dangerous to write about Skye. It is an island that has induced many to compose inordinate sentimentalities and otiose romantic nonsense about it; and temptation persists to add to the rubbish-heap. It can appear to be the very abomination of desolation; or rather non-appear, for it may lie invisible under impacted layers of Atlantic cloud. But while one is damning the topography that pulls in the scourings of every western depression, an errant draught of wind can begin to blow them apart, and within half an hour the Cuillins in their shining splendour rise vast and immaculate against a fleeing wrack that, as it disperses, reveals range upon blue range beyond. Had not a thousand people said so before, one would say, without hesitation, that it is one of the magical places of the earth like Delphi between Parnassus and an intruding finger of the Gulf of Corinth; but to praise a place for being

*The Cuillins of Skye: from Elgol*

*Skye between black cloud and Blackface*

*Bonnie Prince Charlie in 1745*

*The fishing harbour at Mallaig*

*Mouth of the River Morar*

*Glengarry Castle*

*Waterfall on the Morar*

*Boats on the beach at Loch nan Uamh*

*Lichen on a tree branch*

*Heather in flower*

*Sunset over Loch nan Uamh*

# IX

SIR Alexander MacDonald of Sleat, whom the prudent and states-manlike Duncan Forbes of Culloden, Lord President of the Council, had enlisted on the Hanoverian side—Sir Alexander being already of that persuasion—was married to Margaret, one of the seven daughters, famous for their beauty, of Susan, Countess of Eglinton; and the Lady Margaret was a fervent Jacobite.

It had been her habit, while the Prince was on the Long Island, to send newspapers to him by the hand of Hugh MacDonald of Balishair in North Uist—that cousin of Flora's to whose house she had thought of sending the Prince before she agreed to take him to Skye—and when the decision was reached that Skye was where he must go, Balishair wrote to Lady Margaret to say Charles 'wanted all necessaries, particularly shirts.' That letter, and one written in the Prince's own hand, were delivered by Captain Donald Roy MacDonald, who at Culloden had been wounded in the foot, and whose wound was still open. Lady Margaret promptly ordered six of her husband's best shirts to be brought —Sir Alexander was then at Fort Augustus—and finding them dirty, told a chambermaid to have them washed. They were, she said, to be a present to Captain Donald Roy, who had lost all he had on the battlefield. She also changed twenty guineas into smaller money, and gave it to the Captain for the Prince's use.

It was then expected that Charles would land on a small island off the Trotternish peninsula. Donald Roy searched for him in vain, and having returned the shirts and the money to Lady Margaret, retired to his lodging which was only some four miles from her house of Monkstadt, near the beach where the Prince came ashore.

On the 29th June she wrote to Donald Roy to come without loss of time to Monkstadt, for she had matters of the greatest moment to tell him, and wanted his advice. Her messenger ran quickly, and from his landlord—a surgeon called John MacLean—Donald Roy borrowed a horse and rode instantly to Monkstadt. Near the house he saw Lady Margaret walking and earnestly talking to her good factor, MacDonald of Kingsburgh. He dismounted, and Lady Margaret came towards him, hands outspread, and exclaimed, 'O Donald Roy, we are ruined for ever!'

What was the matter? he asked, and woefully she replied that the Prince was on the beach, no more than half a mile away, and if he were to be captured they would be eternally disgraced. What made the situation so extremely difficult was that in her dining-room, at that very moment, was Lieutenant MacLeod of the local militia, whose express duty was to guard the adjacent shore, and particularly to examine every boat coming from the Long Island—and talking to him, in her dining-room, was Flora.

When the fugitives landed, a most unwilling Charles had been left on the beach, where, in his skirt and petticoat and the headdress that made him so uncomfortable, he sat on a trunk. The boatmen had been ordered not to leave the boat, and if any passer-by was inquisitive about the strange appearance of their female companion, he was to be told she was Miss MacDonald's maid, and a lazy creature of little worth, for she did not even bother to attend her mistress. Flora and MacEachain walked to Monkstadt, and Flora asked a servant to let Lady Margaret know that she was on her way to her mother's house, but hoped to see her ladyship before going farther. Her ladyship, as it happened, knew well enough what Flora's business was, for a Mrs. MacDonald of Kirkibost in North Uist, whose husband commanded a militia company, had arrived the day before—her boat having been strictly searched—with the news that Charles was to be expected in Skye very soon.

Lady Margaret deserves sympathy. Jacobite though she was, and immensely concerned for the Prince's safety, she had no wish to compromise her husband, whose loyalty was otherwise engaged; he was still at Fort Augustus. It was fortunate for her that Kingsburgh, her admirable factor, had been dining with her, but Lieutenant MacLeod was a terrible embarrassment; some of his men were in the kitchen or the stables, and the main body not far away. Despite her agitation Lady Margaret disposed of her forces with some acumen.

She persuaded Flora to go in and talk to young MacLeod, she wrote a hurried letter to Donald Roy, and took Kingsburgh to walk in the garden and discuss the situation. She did not want to see the Prince, nor did she. For her husband's sake she had to avoid any personal association with his escape.

Flora, in the meantime, was dealing with the Lieutenant. He and his men, respectable members of the Church of Scotland and sober supporters of the Government, had worshipped God in the morning and in the afternoon may have felt some diminishment of their obligations to His Hanoverian Majesty in London. But Macleod questioned Flora as to who she was, and who had come with her from the Long Island. Her stepfather's name must have reassured him. He was apparently an earnest and dutiful young man, but the languor of a Sunday afternoon may have suggested that his commission did not compel him to search the boat. Flora kept up what she herself called 'a close chit-chat' with him; and it may be inferred that she used all her charm and cleverness to hold him in conversation as long as she could; the visible agitation of Lady Margaret—who kept coming in and going out again—showed that the situation was still dangerous.

In the garden Kingsburgh discussed the possible routes of evasion with Donald Roy. Kingsburgh said there was no safety in Skye, and he thought the Prince should continue his voyage round the point of Trotternish to Raasay. But Lady Margaret rejected that suggestion. Such a course would take him within reach of another militia detachment—stationed on the shore with a boat at hand—and if he were made prisoner there, it would be said that his capture had been pre-arranged. In spite of MacLeod and his men, she thought he must stay where he was till night fell.

Then Donald Roy asked Kingsburgh if he thought it possible to lead the Prince across country to Portree: Portree, on the east coast of Skye, was within easy reach of Raasay. It would be a march of some seventeen or eighteen miles, and Kingsburgh thought it a desperate venture, but it might be tried. He asked Donald Roy to go down to the shore and tell the Prince what they proposed, but Donald Roy, manifestly embarrassed by the prospect of having to talk to such a caricature of womanhood as Charles must present, said that Flora would be a more suitable messenger. Kingsburgh wanted to meet the Prince, but like Donald Roy was unwilling to be seen in company with a grotesquely attired Irish hoyden; and Flora was still engaged with the Lieutenant. In the event it was the ever-serviceable MacEachain who went; and indeed went to and fro so often that Flora grew angry with him for being too obviously busy about something important. No harm was done, however, and Mac-Eachain took the Prince farther down the shore to the back of a little hill, and told him to wait there till Kingsburgh arrived.

Furnishing himself with a bottle of wine and some bread, Kingsburgh set out for the rendezvous, but no Prince was there. Then he noticed a flock of sheep running away, and going to see what had disturbed them found Charles. Though Flora had refused to let him wear a pistol under his petticoat, she had allowed him to carry a useful cudgel, and it was with a lifted cudgel and a menacing question that he greeted Kingsburgh. But when Kingsburgh had identified himself, the Prince became friendly at once and proposed 'jogging on.' It was at Kingsburgh's suggestion that they sat down to drink a little wine and talk about the plan that had been concocted.

It was now decided that the Prince should spend the night at Kingsburgh's house, some seven miles away, and when MacEachain reappeared he was sent back to Monkstadt to ask Flora to meet them on the road and go with them. Donald Roy, with his wounded foot painfully in a stirrup, was already riding in search of the Laird of Raasay's eldest son, who was known as young Rona. Raasay himself had served in the Prince's army, but young Rona, though warmly Jacobite in sympathy, had stayed at home to fabricate an appearance of Hanoverian loyalty and save the estate from confiscation. He or his father, it was thought, would be able to carry the Prince from the island of Raasay to Mackenzie country on the opposite shore of the mainland, which, because of Seaforth's discreet behaviour, was at that time unencumbered by militia-men.

At Monkstadt Lady Margaret had asked Flora to stay with her for some days—Lieutenant MacLeod was still there—but Flora said that in such unsettled times she wanted to be with her mother; and presently set out with Mrs. MacDonald of Kirkibost, her manservant, and her maid, all being mounted. They had not gone far when they overtook Kingsburgh and a companion of curious appearance. Mrs. MacDonald had been let into the secret, and she showed herself uncommonly anxious to get a good look at Betty Burke's face; but the Prince had no reason to trust Mrs. MacDonald's discretion, and whenever she bent down to peer or stare at him, he turned away.

Her maid, observing her curiosity and Betty's strange behaviour, remarked offensively that she had never seen a woman of such impudent appearance, and in her opinion she was either Irish or a man in female dress. She drew attention to Betty's long-striding walk, and a certain clumsiness with which she managed her skirts; and Flora, having assured her that Betty was an Irish woman whom she had known before, thought it advisable to ask Mrs. MacDonald to ride a little faster and leave the pedestrians behind. There was now, it seems, some danger of their meeting parties of militia-men, and the Prince and Kingsburgh were about to leave the road and walk across country; it would be better if the inquisitive maid were not there to see them take to the heather.

As well as the maid, MacEachain had been displeased by the Prince's failure to walk as a woman should. MacEachain had told him, 'For God's sake, Sir, take care what you are doing, for you will certainly discover yourself.'—It was a Sunday evening, there were people on the road, coming home from church, who were astonished to see Kingsburgh walking with so strange a companion. The uncouth-looking woman comported herself with great assurance, and Kingsburgh was most attentive to her, but took little notice of Flora. What greatly shocked the passers-by was to see how Betty Burke, when crossing a little stream, held her skirts indecently aloft.—But to MacEachain's remonstrance the Prince replied with a hearty laugh, thanked him for his concern, and when they came to another stream let his petticoat trail in the water.

Somewhere on the road Flora parted from Mrs. MacDonald of Kirkibost and her servants, and reached Kingsburgh House a little while before the pedestrians. It was between ten and eleven o'clock when they arrived, the Prince much fatigued. Mrs. MacDonald—Kingsburgh's wife, that is—was about to go to bed, not expecting to see her husband that night, when a maid told her that Kingsburgh had come home and brought some company with him. What happened next is told exactly as related by Bishop Forbes—of whom more will be said later—he having heard the story from Kingsburgh and his wife in Leith, in July, 1747.

' "What company?" says Mrs. MacDonald.

' "Milton's daughter, I believe," says the maid, "and some company with her."

' "Milton's daughter," replies Mrs. MacDonald, "is very welcome to come here with any company she pleases to bring. But you'll give my service to her, and tell her to make free with anything in the house; for I am very sleepy and cannot see her this night."

'In a little her own daughter came and told her in a surprize, "O mother, my father has brought in a very odd, muckle, ill-shaken-up wife as ever I saw! I never saw the like of her, and he has gone into the hall with her."

'She had scarce done with telling her tale when Kingsburgh came and desired his lady to fasten on her bucklings again, and to get some supper for him and the company he had brought with him.

' "Pray, goodman," says she, "what company is this you have brought with you?"

' "Why, goodwife," said he, "you shall know that in due time; only make haste and get some supper in the meantime."

'Mrs. MacDonald desired her daughter to go and fetch her the keys she had left in the hall. When her daughter came to the door of the hall, she started back, ran to her mother and told her she could not go in for the keys, for the muckle woman was walking up and down in the hall, and she was so frighted at seeing her that she could not have the courage to enter. Mrs. Macdonald went herself to get the keys, and I heard her more than once declare that upon looking in at the door she had not the courage to go forward.

' "For," said she, "I saw such an odd muckle trallup of a carlin, making lang wide steps through the hall that I could not like her appearance at all."

'Mrs. MacDonald called Kingsburgh, and very seriously begged to know what a lang, odd hussie was this he had brought to the house; for that she was so frighted at the sight of her that she could not go into the hall for her keys.

' "Did you never see a woman before," said he, "goodwife? What frights you at seeing a woman? Pray, make haste, and get us some supper."

'Kingsburgh would not go for the keys, and therefore his lady behov'd to go for them. When she entered the hall, the Prince happen'd to be sitting; but immediately he arose, went forward and saluted Mrs. MacDonald, who, feeling a long stiff beard, trembled to think that this behoved to be some distressed nobleman or gentleman in disguise, for she never dream'd it to be the Prince, though all along she had been seized with a dread she could not account for from the moment she had heard that Kingsburgh had brought company with him. She very soon made out of the hall with her keys, never saying one word. Immediately she importun'd Kingsburgh to tell her who the person was, for that she was sure by the salute that it was some distressed gentleman.

'Kingsburgh smiled at the mention of the bearded kiss, and said: "Why, my dear, it is the Prince. You have the honour to have him in your house."

' "The Prince," cried she. "O Lord, we are a' ruin'd and undone for ever! We will a' be hang'd now!"

' "Hout, goodwife," says the honest stout soul, "we will die but ance; and if we are hanged for this, I am sure we die in a good cause. Pray, make no delay; go, get some supper. Fetch what is readiest. You have eggs and butter and cheese in the house, get them as quickly as possible."

' "Eggs and butter and cheese!" says Mrs. MacDonald, "what a supper is that for a Prince?"

' "O goodwife," said he, "little do you know how this good Prince has been living for some time past. These, I can assure you, will be a feast to him. Besides, it would be unwise to be dressing a formal supper, because this would serve to raise the curiosity of the servants, and they would be making their observations. The less ceremony and work the better. Make haste and see that you come to supper."

' "I come to supper!" says Mrs. MacDonald; "how can I come to supper? I know not how to behave before Majesty."

' "You must come," says Kingsburgh, "for he will not eat a bit till he see you at the table; and you will find it no difficult matter to behave before him, so obliging and easy is he in his conversation."

'The Prince ate of our roasted eggs, some collops, plenty of bread and butter, etc., and (to use the words of Mrs. MacDonald) "the deel a drap did he want in's weam of twa bottles of sma beer. God do him good o't; for, well I wat, he had my blessing to gae down wi't."

'After he had made a plentiful supper, he called for a dram; and when the bottle of brandy was brought, he said he would fill the glass for himself; "for," said he, "I have learn'd in my skulking to take a hearty dram." He filled up a bumper and drank it off to the happiness and prosperity of his landlord and landlady. Then taking a crack'd and broken pipe out of his poutch, wrapt about with thread, he asked Kingsburgh if he could furnish him with some tobacco; for that he had learn'd likewise to smoke in his wanderings. Kingsburgh took from him the broken pipe and laid it carefully up with the brogs (his shoes, that is) and gave him a new clean pipe and plenty of tobacco.

'The Prince and Kingsburgh turn'd very familiar and merry together, and when the Prince spoke to Kingsburgh, he for the most part laid his hand upon Kingsburgh's knee and used several kind and obliging expressions in his conversation with the happy landlord. Kingsburgh remarked what a lucky thing it was that he happened to be at Monkstadt (Sir Alexander MacDonald's house), and that it was all a matter of chance that he was there, for he had no design of being there that day. And then he asked the Prince what he would have done if he had not been at Monkstadt.

'The Prince replied, "Why, sir, you could not avoid being at Monkstadt this day; for Providence ordered you to be there on my account."

'Kingsburgh became so merry and jocose that putting up his hand to the Prince's face, he turned off his head-dress which was a very odd clout of a mutch or toy; upon which Mrs. MacDonald hasted out of the room and brought a clean nightcap for him.

'Both Kingsburgh and his lady said that the Prince's face and hands were very much sun-burnt. But they declared he had not a spot of the itch upon him, though a silly report had been raised by his malicious enemies that he was scabbed to the eye-holes. His legs, they said, were hacked in some parts, which was occasioned by his walking and sleeping so often in wet hose. Mrs. MacDonald used the freedom to put up the sleeve of his gown and of his shirt (a very coarse dud), "and there," said she, "I saw a bonny, clean, white skin indeed. The deel a lady in a' the land has a whiter and purer skin than he has." '

The narrative continues: 'After Miss Flora had got up, Mrs. Mac-Donald told her that she wanted much to have a lock of the Prince's hair, and that she behoved to go into his room and get it for her. Miss

Flora refused to do as she desired, because the Prince was not yet out of bed.

' "What then," said Mrs. MacDonald, "no harm will happen to you. He is too good to harm you or any person. You must instantly go in and get me the lock."

'Mrs. MacDonald, taking hold of Miss with one hand, knocked at the door of the room with the other. The Prince called, "Who is there?"

'Mrs. MacDonald, opening the door, said, "Sir, it is I, and I am importuneing Miss Flora to come in and get a lock of your hair to me, and she refuses to do it."

' "Pray," said the Prince, "desire Miss MacDonald to come in. What should make her afraid to come where I am?"

'When Miss came in he begged her to sit down on a chair at the bedside, then laying his arms about her waist, and his head upon her lap, he desired her to cut out the lock with her own hands in token of future and more substantial favours. The one half of the lock Miss gave to Mrs. MacDonald and the other she kept to herself. I heard Mrs. MacDonald say that when Miss Flora at any time happened to come into the room where the Prince was, he always rose from his seat, paid her the same respects as if she had been a queen, and made her sit on his right hand.'

It was late in the day when the ladies cut a lock of hair from the Prince's head, for he and Kingsburgh had sat long over their punch, and slept soundly. But at breakfast they resumed their conversation, and the Prince told his host that although he had found Lord George Murray difficult to deal with, he would never accuse him of treachery. During his wanderings in the Outer Isles he had often spoken angrily about Murray, and complained of his ill temper; but treachery was another matter, and of that Murray had not been guilty. It became evident that Charles was by no means willing to leave the comfort of Kingsburgh House—for the first time since Culloden he had slept between sheets—but Kingsburgh was anxious about his guest's safety,

*Decanter and wine-glass for the drinking Jacobite*

and went to some trouble to explain to him the danger and inconveniency of his going in female dress. 'You are very bad,' he said, 'at acting the part of a dissembler.' For the servants' sake he must leave the house as Betty Burke, but somewhere on the road he should stop and change into highland costume; and that, with a broadsword to his hand, 'would become him much better.'

Kingsburgh's daughter Nannie was married to a husband who favoured the Hanoverian interest, and he, though in the house, had kept, or been kept, discreetly out of the way. But Nannie felt free to rob his wardrobe, and found a suit which fitted the Prince very well; and Nannie, said her mother, must help him to put on Betty Burke's clothes. 'For,' said she, 'the deel a preen he could put in.'

So, with great hilarity, the Prince was again dressed as a woman; and after 'gown, hood, mantle etc., were put on, he said, "Oh, Miss, you have forgot my apron. Where is my apron? Pray get me my apron here, for that is a principal part of my dress."

'Kingsburgh and his lady both declared that the Prince behaved not like one that was in danger, but as chearfully and merrily as if he had been putting on women's cloathes merely for a piece of diversion.'

It was not until late in the day that he left, after dining, drinking tea, and some glasses of wine. Flora, with MacEachain for escort, had left earlier, apparently to go to her mother's house at Armadale in the far south of the island; but for some unknown reason—she may well have been tired—they stopped at the inn in Portree. Charles's last recorded words in Kingsburgh's hospitable house, of which no stone remains, were, 'Can none of you give me a snuff?' Mrs. MacDonald brought him 'a little silver mill with two hands clasped together upon the lid of it', and Kingsburgh begged him to keep it as a remembrance. Then they sat out together, and at the edge of a wood, not far from the house, the Prince changed into highland dress. Betty Burke's uncomfortable clothes were hidden in a bush, but not left there for long. The cotton gown, which was lilac-sprigged, Mrs. MacDonald made into a bedcover, and Flora got the apron. Other garments, carefully retrieved, had to be burnt as carefully when soldiers came to search for evidence of the Prince's sojourn in the house.

He took sad farewell of Kingsburgh, and with a small boy called MacQueen for his guide walked through the darkness towards Portree. It was the last day of June, and raining again. At the inn in Portree Captain Donald Roy MacDonald had found Flora and MacEachain, and told them that with young Rona's help he had made arrangements for the Prince's little voyage to Raasay. Flora asked him to go out and wait for the Prince, but it was now raining heavily, and after some time his wounded foot became so painful that he had to go in. Then Macnab, the landlord, told him that a boy had come with a message for him, and MacQueen said a gentleman was waiting outside to talk to him. The Prince greeted Donald Roy with a great show of affection, and Donald Roy deplored the wild weather through which he had had to walk. But the Prince said only that he was sorry 'our lady had been abused with the rain.'

They went into the inn, and the Prince, with water dripping from his kilt or belted plaid, took a dram standing. The boy came in again to say that Donald Roy was wanted, and now he went out to find Captain Malcolm MacLeod, a cousin of the Laird of Raasay who had fought at Culloden. Young Rona had asked him for help, and he was overjoyed to be of assistance. Rona and his younger brother, with a couple of boatmen, were waiting, he said, to take the Prince over to Raasay, and it would be well for them to start at once, while the rain was falling and the night was dark. But Donald Roy was mindful of the Prince's comfort, who was drenched already, and brought whisky for the boat's crew to persuade them to wait patiently. Captain Malcolm went back to the boat, and in the inn Donald Roy begged the Prince to put on a dry shirt. He was, for once, well supplied with both food and clothing, for Kingsburgh had given him four shirts, a cold hen, a bottle of brandy, and half a loaf of sugar.

*The pier at Portree*

Because Flora was with them in the room, the Prince was unwilling to strip and change, but Donald Roy and MacEachain told him it was no time for ceremony, and Donald Roy offered him his kilt. The Prince had already ordered a meal of roasted fish, bread and butter and cheese, and sitting down in his dry shirt, and nothing else, ate heartily. It was a scene that made Donald Roy smile, and when the Prince asked him why, he said, 'I believe, Sir, that is the English fashion.' 'What fashion do you mean?' says the Prince. 'Why,' replied the Captain, 'they say the English, when they are to eat heartily, throw off their cloaths.' Too tactful to ask where Donald Roy had acquired this uncommon knowledge of the convivial habits of South Britain, the Prince agreed that it was practical. 'They are in the right,' he said, 'lest anything should incommode their hands when they are at work.'

Unwilling, as it seems, to open his bottle of brandy, he enquired what drink there was in the inn. Only whisky or water, he was told; for in all the Isle of Skye beer and ale were to be found only in gentlemen's houses. He asked for milk, but there was none. He must drink water, said Donald Roy, and offered him an ugly vessel that the innkeeper used for bailing out his boat. He had just drunk from it himself, and when he saw the Prince look doubtfully at it he whispered—for the innkeeper was in the room—that he must not show untimely delicacy for fear of rousing suspicion. So the Prince took a hearty draught, and finished dressing in clothes which, by then, might be half-dry.

Donald Roy was anxious for him to be gone; the inn was a public place, and none knew who might come in. But the rain was still pouring down, and the Prince wanted to stay the night in Portree. He was persuaded that it would be unwise, and to put off departure called for tobacco. Only a coarse, roll tobacco was to be got, but the Prince said that would serve him very well, and Donald Roy told the innkeeper to fetch a quarter of a pound; which cost fourpence ha'penny. The Prince gave him sixpence, and Donald Roy asked for the change. The Prince was amused at such carefulness, but Donald Roy sensibly said that in his present situation he might find bawbees very useful; so the Prince put them in his purse.

The innkeeper left them, and the Prince began to plead with Donald Roy to come with him to Raasay. He knew little or nothing of the MacLeods to whom he must now entrust himself—they were strangers belonging to a clan whose chief had shown him no friendship—and he had grown used to reliance on the stalwart loyalty of the many Mac-Donalds who had succoured him. But Donald Roy said he would be more hindrance than help, for his wounded foot would not let him walk far, he needed a horse to carry him, and a mounted man in attendance would be too conspicuous. He spoke of their plan to send him, as soon as possible, into Mackenzie country on the mainland, and the Prince asked whom he knew of the Mackenzies. None, he said, but old Raasay knew them well.

It was indeed an agonising leave-taking that Charles had now to face, and only the righteous will be shocked to hear that he and Donald Roy and MacEachain drank a bottle of whisky between them before he finally left the inn. Of Flora's part in the conversation there is no record. She was in the room when Charles changed his shirt, and presumably there while the men argued, and bought tobacco, and drank their whisky; but perhaps, in a Highland fashion, she had been taught to sit quiet while fathers, husbands, brothers, and male cousins did the talking. Charles was always respectful to her, but even he may have become so much a Highlander that he paid her scant attention when masculine discussion seemed more interesting. Again he asked Donald Roy to go with him to Raasay—'I am anxious to have a MacDonald along with me' —but Donald Roy, with his crippled foot, wisely refused; and took the chance to speak a good word for his chief. 'Though Sir Alexander and his following did not join Your Royal Highness,' he said, 'yet you see you have been very safe amongst them; for though they did not repair to your standard, they wish you very well.'

The Prince had to pay his reckoning, and wanted change for a

guinea. The innkeeper had only eleven shillings, and Charles was willing to take that, but Donald Roy would not let him. Such extravagance would certainly rouse suspicion, and he found the small money that was needed. If the Prince required more, he said, he was sure the Lady Margaret would help him; but the Prince—a little stiffly because she had avoided meeting him—said that although he was much obliged to her, he did not wish to be troublesome to any of his friends in that way.

He remembered a small debt to Flora, and gave her half a crown that he owed her. He took farewell of her, saluted her, and with a royal condescension replacing the familiarity they had enjoyed together, told her, 'For all that has happened I hope, Madam, we shall meet in St. James's yet.' But she never saw him again.

It was, perhaps, the ideal farewell; for she had served him as if he were her king, and as her king he left her. His accoutrements, however, were something less than royal, for as he went from the inn he had a bottle of whisky tied to his belt at one side, and on the other, in a napkin, Kingsburgh's bottle of brandy, four shirts, and a cold hen. MacEachain stayed with Flora, and the Prince and Donald Roy took a circuitous route to the boat, for the innkeeper came out to see which way they went. To Captain Malcolm MacLeod and the two young MacLeods his cousins, Donald Roy said he would remain in Skye to learn what he could of the enemy's knowledge of the Prince's movements, and it was agreed that he and young Rona would meet on the following Thursday.

There was a last moment of rather absurd sentimentality when the Prince took from his pocket the half-loaf of sugar that Kingsburgh had given him, and asked Donald Roy to take it to 'our lady'. 'For I am afraid,' he said, 'she will get no sugar where she is going.'

Donald Roy privily returned the sugar to Captain Malcolm, and about dawn on Tuesday, the 1st July, the Prince went aboard the boat, which headed out for Raasay.

# X

PURSUIT, which had narrowly missed Charles, closed in upon his friends. The boatmen who had brought him and Flora to Skye had returned immediately to South Uist: so Flora told Mrs. MacDonald while she was at Kingsburgh House. 'I wish,' said Mrs. MacDonald, 'you had sunk the boat and kept the boatmen in Skye where they could have been concealed, and then we would have known the better what to have done with the Prince, because his enemies by this means would have lost scent of him. But all will be wrong by their returning to South Uist.'

'I hope not,' said Flora, 'for we took care to depone them before they parted from us.'

'Alas!' replied Mrs. MacDonald, 'your deponing of them will not signify a farthing. For if once the military get hold of them they will terrify them out of their senses and make them forget their oath.'

And so it happened. As soon as they landed in South Uist the boatmen were made prisoners, and threatened with torture unless they told all they knew. They did not resist. They described the manner of the Prince's escape and the disguise he wore, even to the colour of his lilac-sprigged dress. Nor should they be greatly blamed, for they knew he would not wear Betty Burke's petticoats a moment longer than was necessary.

Donald Roy, after sleeping all morning at the inn in Portree, rode to Kingsburgh with news of the Prince's departure, and from there to Monkstadt. He met and was made welcome by Lieutenant MacLeod, who insisted that Donald Roy should spend the night with him. He discovered, to his relief, that MacLeod had heard nothing of the Prince having been in Skye, but thought he was still in the Long Island. The unhappy boatmen, however, had told of his escape, and a few days later Captain Ferguson, having already searched Sir Alexander MacDonald's house, came to Kingsburgh. The good man of Kingsburgh told his wife that the Captain had come to examine her about some lodgers she had lately had in her house, and 'desired her to be distinct in her answers.'

Mrs. MacDonald was unabashed. She looked the brutal officer full in the face and said, 'If Captain Ferguson is to be my judge, then God have mercy upon my soul.'

Ferguson asked why she spoke in such a fashion.

'Why, sir,' said Mrs. MacDonald, 'the world belies you if you be not a very cruel, hard-hearted man.'

Not used to being addressed so rudely, Ferguson had nothing better to say than 'People should not believe all the world says.'

He asked Kingsburgh where Miss MacDonald and 'the person along with her in woman's cloaths' had slept.

'I know in what room Miss MacDonald herself lay,' said Kingsburgh, 'but where servants are laid when in my house, I know nothing of that matter, I never enquire anything about it. My wife is the properest person to inform you about that.'

Ferguson, with singular coarseness, ordered Mrs. MacDonald to tell him, 'Whether or not you laid the young Pretender and Miss MacDonald in one bed.'

To which she answered, 'Sir, whom you mean by the young Pretender I shall not pretend to guess; but I can assure you it is not the fashion in the Isle of Skye to lay the mistress and the maid in the same bed together.'

But Ferguson demanded to see the rooms where her lodgers had slept, and said sourly that it was pretty remarkable that the room which the maid had been given seemed to look better than that where the mistress had slept.

Kingsburgh was arrested and sent to Fort Augustus, where his guards stole his watch, his money, and his silver shoe-buckles. Later he was removed to Edinburgh Castle, where for a year he lay in prison.

Donald Roy, after a night in Lieutenant MacLeod's company, had gone again to Monkstadt, walking four miles in great pain with his wounded foot in a cloth shoe, and there provided himself with a pocket-pistol and a good dirk. Lady Margaret wrote a letter to the Prince, wishing him all happiness and offering him such help as was in her power to give; and Donald Roy undertook to deliver it. Borrowing a horse, he rode to Kingsburgh and there found a boy who would run beside him and take the horse back from his next port-of-call; which was a house called Tottrome, near Portree, where young Rona's sister lived. There young Rona came out to meet him with the news that the Prince, having returned to Skye, was sleeping in a cow-byre not far away. It was now the 3rd July.

By the time Donald Roy got to the byre, the Prince had left; and later they failed to meet at Camastianavaig, south of Portree, where the Prince had appointed a rendezvous with young Murdoch. But there Donald Roy was given a letter which read: 'Sir,—I have parted (I thank God) as intended. Make my compliments to all those to whom I have given trouble.—I am, Sir, your humble servant, James Thomson.'

At Camastianavaig—or perhaps from young Rona—he borrowed another horse and rode to the house of Flora's mother at Armadale. Flora had arrived there safely after a very tiring journey across country, and told her mother nothing of her recent activity. On the 9th or 10th July, while Donald Roy was still there, Flora was given a letter which told her that Captain John MacLeod of Talisker, an officer in the militia, wanted to see her. She still had the compromising letter, with its recommendation of Betty Burke, which her stepfather had written when he procured a passport for her; and Donald Roy had Lady Margaret's letter and that signed by 'James Thomson'. These two he burnt, and made Flora give him the other before she obeyed her summons. No attempt to evade it would have succeeded, for on the road she met a party of soldiers, by whom she was arrested and taken aboard Captain Ferguson's sloop *Furness*. Luckily for her, General Campbell was also aboard, and by his orders she was treated with all respect.

Donald Roy was more fortunate. He took to the heather and avoided capture. He was a formidable fellow, six feet in height, and tolerably well armed with the pocket-pistol and the good dirk he had been given at Monkstadt. His wound, presumably, was now healing, and to occupy his mind he composed Latin poetry.

# XI

IN his reluctance to leave Portree the Prince had shown considerable prescience, for Raasay offered him no refuge. About a month after Culloden it had been plundered and burnt—pillaged without mercy and hideously devastated—by order of that most abominable officer of the Royal Navy, Captain Ferguson. The Laird's own house was burnt to ashes, and by his son's estimate more than three hundred cottages were destroyed: every habitation on the island, except for two little clachans that escaped notice, was left in ruins. A Lieutenant Dalrymple, one of Ferguson's officers, marched through the island with sailors, marines, and militia-men in three bodies, who slaughtered all the animals in their path: not for the harness-cask, but for punishment. They left the carcases to rot. And worse befell the wretched islanders a few weeks later, when news arrived of the Prince's escape from the Long Island. By then, it seems, a very fury of hatred, of the Prince and all who supported or might support him, had infected his enemies; for on the written testimony of John MacLeod—young Rona, the heir of Raasay—men of a punitive force on the little, rocky island of Rona, just north of Raasay, raped a blind girl and flogged two men so brutally that one died of their lashes and the other never fully recovered; while on Raasay itself the remnant poor were robbed of the clothes they wore, their surviving cattle were ruthlessly killed, and two named women were raped, one of whom 'walked upon stilts'. It was to that scene of blackened horror—but before the second punishment—that Charles fled from Portree on a morning of continuous rain.

Against that picture must be set the joyous devotion of the young men of the house of Raasay—Rona and his brother Murdoch, who had been shot through the shoulder at Culloden, and their imperturbable cousin, Captain Malcolm—of them, and the loyal servants who helped them—and if it be argued that the whole enterprise showed little judgment, the answer is that the Prince's situation was so enclosed by danger that no certain way of escape was visible, and in such conditions enthusiasm may well be injudicious.

In the boat that took him to the devastated island the Prince quickly became familiar with his new-found adherents, and told them—with a platitude such as crises induce—that 'friends who showed their friendship in distress were the real friends.' About daybreak they landed at Glam on the west shore of Raasay, and went to a hut so small that he had to stoop to enter it. Murdoch MacLeod went off to look for food, and came back with a young kid in his plaid, and oat-bread and butter. The kid was killed and stewed, and Charles ate heartily; for danger never destroyed his appetite. He was so pleasant as to say he preferred oat-bread to the biscuits he carried. 'This,' he declared, 'is my own country bread.'

But he enquired very closely about the depredations the island had suffered, and was much affected by the dreadful stories he was told. There would be better days to come, he said, and he would see to it that all the ruined turf-cottages were replaced with stone-built houses. He walked to and fro on a green near the wretched hut, and said that his own recent life, in a small way, could be called hard, but he would rather have ten years of such an existence than be taken by his enemies; and marvelled a little at the strength he had shown. 'For since Culloden,' he said, 'I have endured more than would kill a hundred. Sure Providence does not design this for nothing.'

Wholly unconcerned, as it appeared, he sat down to supper, and a couple of servants having been posted as sentries, lay down to sleep with the wounded Murdoch and the redoubtable Captain Malcolm on either side. In the morning, however, when young Rona said he must keep his appointment in Skye with Donald Roy, the Prince said he would go with him; and the others agreed, deciding that nine o'clock at night would be a suitable hour for their departure. It is pretty evident that one or other of the party had reconnoitred the island, and after that their conversation had been realistic: they had come to the conclusion that Raasay could neither shelter the Prince nor give him access to any place of safety.

While they were talking, one of their faithful servants came in to say there was a travelling man, a pedlar, who seemed to be approaching their hut. He was a man, known by sight, who had earlier been suspected of spying for the Government. The young MacLeods thought that if he came near enough to recognise the Prince he should, as a measure of safety, be killed. But to that the Prince would not agree, saying 'God forbid that we should take any poor man's life while we can save our own.' And to save further argument the pedlar passed by at a safe distance.

When the time came to put to sea, the weather was again bad, with 'a pretty high wind, and a very rainy night.' The boat was small, the wind increased to gale force. In the boat with the Prince were young Rona, his brother Murdoch, Captain Malcolm, and the two boatmen who had ferried them to Raasay; both of whom had served in his army. The short passage was not without danger, for the waves broke high over the boat and Captain Malcolm was kept hard at work bailing. But the Prince would not hear of turning back, and sang cheerfully while the rowers tugged at their oars. It was nine or ten o'clock at night when they landed at Nicolson's Rock, on the north side of Portree harbour, and in the difficult business of going ashore on a ragged, weed-hung coast the Prince was as active as any, though encumbered by a long, salt-water-sodden coat.

They walked a little way to the north, and found shelter in a cow-byre, where they had a scanty supper of cheese and oat-bread broken down to crumbs. The Prince was restless, and slept little. In the morning he said good-bye to the two young MacLeods and their boatmen, promising—for no very clear reason—to meet Murdoch at Camastiana-vaig. He expected, he said, to see Donald Roy, but in the early evening, before Donald Roy had come, he left the byre and Captain Malcolm followed him.

He walked, at first, rather aimlessly. It was not until he had taken a path which might lead him into danger that Captain Malcolm asked

*The burn of Sligachan in Skye*

where he wanted to go, and the Prince replied that he hoped to reach Strath, the country of the old chief of the Mackinnons. This new project had been conceived, presumably, in the course of conversation in the hut on Raasay; and however well advised, presented some difficulty. The Prince told Malcolm, 'Why, MacLeod, I now throw myself entirely into your hands, and leave you to do with me what you please.' But when Malcolm said he would take him to Mackinnon's country easily enough if he would consent to go by sea—which would be safer by far than going across country—the Prince refused, and said he meant to walk. He knew the way, he said.

Captain Malcolm replied that he probably knew it better; and they were faced with a long walk. As much as thirty miles, perhaps, for they could not always choose a direct path, but for safety must use byways. Nor did he want to walk by night, for if any harm befell the Prince, he would be held responsible. But the Prince was obdurate, and 'away they went along the ridges of high hills, and through wild muirs and glens.' It was decided that Charles should pretend to be the Captain's servant, and take the name of Lewie Caw; which was, in fact, the name of a young surgeon who at that time was also in hiding. To play the part realistically Charles was to walk a little distance behind Captain Malcolm; and he insisted on carrying their scanty baggage.

From a little way north of Portree harbour their route would be west of the village, west of the sandy loch of Portree and down the long ten miles of Glen Varragill—through which runs the modern road—nearly as far as the head of Loch Sligachan. But Sligachan was occupied by the enemy, and there they would have to make another detour to the west. It was three days before the new moon, which did not rise till after midnight, but nights are still short in the first days of July, and if the sky was clear they would have seen ahead of them the dark, shapely bulk of Marsco rising between the Cuillins and the hills of Lord MacDonald's Forest. With Sligachan safely behind them it was over or round the heights of the Forest they went next—crossing, perhaps, the saddle between Marsco and Ben Dearg—and so downhill to the shore of Loch Ainort, and along the shore till Strath Mor began to open. Then down the Strath to the head of Loch Slapin and a line that is now shown by the road from there to Elgol. They reached Elgol in the early morning, after walking for twelve hours or longer; and there, if the day was fine, they may have been gratified by the broad view across Loch Scavaig to Soay and the great ridge of the Cuillins.

They had had time for a good deal of conversation, for on such a walk, in such conditions, they must from time to time have had to sit and watch till some moving figure had gone his way, or a dog stopped barking; and again the vexatious character of Lord George Murray was discussed. For two or three days before Culloden, said the Prince, Murray had scarcely done anything he asked him to do. From Captain Malcolm he heard, for the first time, stories of the cruelty that had followed the battle, and found it difficult to believe that Cumberland could have countenanced such barbarism. Charles had the bad habit of drinking hill-water when he was warm and sweating, and when Captain Malcolm warned him that it was a dangerous practice, he defended it with an item of folk-medicine—with the sort of popular therapy that used to be cherished by sailors and time-serving soldiers of a vanished generation—and answered, 'No, no, that will never hurt me in the least. If you happen to drink any cold thing when you are warm, only remember, MacLeod, to piss after drinking, and it will do you no harm at all. This advice I had from a friend abroad.'

He walked very quickly and made light of fatigue; and between them they finished a bottle of brandy before reaching Elgol. When dawn had broken Captain Malcolm saw that the Prince was uneasy and fidgeting, and having persuaded him to sit down and open the breast of his shirt, saw that he was lousy. There was no cause for surprise in the discovery—infection could have come either from the hut on Raasay or the cow-byre beyond Portree—but the Prince, uncomplaining as usual, had never thought to grumble at his discomfort, though lice are abominably irritating; and one hopes that he walked more easily after Captain Malcolm had removed an estimated fourscore from his body.

As they approached Mackinnon's country, Malcolm advised him to do something to improve his thin disguise as a servant; for Mackinnon and his men had been out in the rebellion, and he might well be recognised. Should he blacken his face? asked the Prince. But Malcolm did not recommend so extreme a device. Then the Prince pulled off his periwig, stuffed it into a pocket, and found a dirty napkin that he asked Malcolm to tie on his head in such a way that it would come low down over his eyes. He put on his bonnet above the napkin, and felt confident that he could now pass anywhere as a servant, and one, moreover, exhausted by hard work. Malcolm was still doubtful, and the Prince exclaimed. 'This is an odd remarkable face I have got that nothing can disguise it!' The real difficulty, as Malcolm later declared, was that he could never 'dissemble his air'. Whatever he wore, one could not fail to 'see something about him that was not ordinary, something of the stately and the grand.' Almost immediately, indeed, they met a couple of Mackinnon's men who had been 'out', and they, seeing the Prince in such straits, 'lifted their hands and wept bitterly.'

At Elgol lived Malcolm's sister, married to Captain John Mackinnon. Her husband was away from home, and Malcolm told his sister that he had come to stay for a little while, and had with him a servant called Lewie Caw; who was brought in with their luggage in a pack on his back and the napkin round his head. He took off his bonnet, made a low bow, and sat down at some distance from his master. There was something about the lad, said Malcolm's sister, that she liked 'unco well'; and she admired his looks. When bread and cheese and milk were set before Malcolm, he told Lewie to come and take his share; but Lewie, pretending to be shy, said he knew his manners better than that, and obeyed reluctantly.

During the night march the Prince had fallen into a bog, almost to the top of his thighs—and he was wearing a philabeg, the small kilt—

and Malcolm, in pulling him out, had himself been bogged. There was a servant girl in the house, who spoke only Gaelic, and Malcolm asked her to bring a tub of water to wash his feet and legs. While she was busy with him, he said to her, 'You see that poor sick man there? I hope you'll wash his feet too.'

'No such thing,' she said. 'Although I wash the master's feet, I am not obliged to wash the servant's. What! He's nothing but a low countrywoman's son.'

But Malcolm, with some difficulty, persuaded her to wash Lewie's feet, and the girl, in reprisal for such humiliation, went roughly about her task. Said the Prince to Malcolm, 'Oh, MacLeod, would you desire the girl not to go so far up?'

They both got a little sleep while Malcolm's sister kept watch, sitting on a knowe not far from the house. When she saw her husband approaching, Malcolm was wakened and went out to meet him. There were ships of war in Loch Scavaig, and Captain Malcolm said to Captain John, 'What if our Prince be aboard one of them?'

'God forbid,' said Captain John. 'I would not wish that for anything.'

'What if we had him here, John? Do you think he would be in safety?'

'I wish with all my heart we had him here,' said John, 'for he would be safe enough.'

'Well, then, he is here already. He is just now in your house.'

Captain John Mackinnon, that admirable man, appears to have heard such alarming news with remarkable equanimity, but when he went indoors—though he had been warned to respect the Prince's disguise—he could not keep from staring at him. The Prince himself had evidently forgotten his assumed character. He was playing with a small son of the house, carrying him in his arms and singing to him, and with a bland indifference to his being *incognito*, said, 'I hope this child may be a captain in my service yet.' At which Captain John turned his face away and wept.

There was discussion about finding a boat that would take Charles to the mainland, and it was decided to say nothing about his presence to the old Laird of Mackinnon; who, though 'a mighty honest, stout, good man', was old and infirm. The best plan, it was thought, would be for Captain John to engage a boatman to carry Malcolm, saying nothing about another passenger; and off he went to fulfil that purpose. but on the road he met his chief, and was so full of what he had to do that he could not contain it. Whereupon the old Mackinnon took all responsibility upon himself, and declared his intention of coming to pay his respects to the Prince.

On hearing that, Captain Malcolm sensibly resolved to say good-bye to Charles and let the old Mackinnon take charge of him. The chief, it is evident, was a man who did not suffer gladly any dissenting opinion, and if Malcolm should differ from him there would only be trouble. The Prince was unwilling to let him go, but when Malcolm said that his absence from home might already have roused suspicion—there might be search-parties out for him who would endanger them both—he agreed reluctantly to the new proposal.

The old chief arrived, having lost no time in ordering a boat, and about eight or nine at night they all went down to the shore. As he was about to step into the boat the Prince said to Malcolm, 'Don't you remember that I promised to meet Murdoch MacLeod at'—he paused, and could not remember the name of Camastianavaig—'at such a place?'

'No matter,' said Malcolm, 'I shall make your apology.'

'That's not enough,' said the Prince. 'Have you paper, pen, and ink upon you, MacLeod? I'll write him a few lines. I'm obliged so to do in good manners.'

That Malcolm habitually carried paper, pen, and ink seems unlikely, and it is probable that the others waited while he or Captain John ran to the house and back again. Then, on a thwart of the boat, the Prince wrote to Murdoch MacLeod of Raasay the letter that he signed 'Your humble servant, James Thomson'; the letter that was given to Donald Roy.

*The dance continues*

There was a brief altercation when some ships hove into sight, and appeared to be making in their direction. Malcolm begged the Prince to wait awhile before embarking, for the ships were sailing with the wind behind them, and might cut him off. But the Prince would not hear of delay. The wind was about to change, he said, and the ships would go off on a contrary course: 'Providence will take care of me, and it will not be in the power of these ships to look near me at this time.' The wind, indeed, changing almost immediately, 'blew pretty briskly', and the hostile ships were soon out of sight. Malcolm was much impressed by such prescience, and one may infer that during his stormy voyaging off the Long Island Charles had acquired, not only trust in Providence, but some useful weather lore.

Malcolm's last service to him was to help him light a cutty pipe. With its clay stem broken off short, the bowl of the pipe lay almost against the Prince's cheek. Malcolm took a piece of tow from his pocket, held it to the pan of a gun, snapped the gun, and kindled the tow. He put the tow to the tobacco, and while the Prince sucked, he blew. The tow flared, and scarred the Prince's cheek; but Malcolm got a silver stock-buckle for a keepsake, and ten guineas—forced upon him against his wish—as a more useful token of regard.

# XII

THE boat put out on its short voyage past Strathaird Point, across the mouth of Loch Eishort to the Point of Sleat, and so across the Sound of Sleat to Mallaig. Aboard with the Prince were the old Mackinnon, Captain John, and four men to row. They landed in the early morning of the 5th July, and found either a deserted or a frightened countryside. There was a militia encampment at Earnsaig on the south side of the entrance to Loch Nevis, and for three days and nights the Prince and his companions could find none able or willing to shelter them. They lay in the open, and on the fourth morning the old laird, taking one of the boatmen, went off to look for quarters that would give them, at least, a roof over their heads.

In his absence the Prince, Captain John, and the other three boatmen launched the boat and made what seems to have been a reckless reconnaissance into Loch Nevis. Rounding a point on its shore, they saw a boat tied to a rock, and near it five men 'with red crosses over their bonnets', who ordered them to come in and land. The Prince was willing to do so, but Captain John took command, and they pulled away. Charles was down on the bottom-boards, covered by a plaid—this at Captain John's insistence—and the boatmen, who were armed, had their muskets ready but strict orders not to fire until ordered. The Prince said there was to be no needless bloodshed, and Captain John agreed; with the prudent addition that if they did open fire, they must see to it that none of their pursuers escaped. They were making, he said, for a part of the shore where there was good cover, and the militia-men would not follow.

The five men, in their boat, had quickly followed, but were out-rowed, and beyond another foreland the fugitives put in to the wooded shore. The Prince, with Captain John and one of the boatmen, ran quickly to the top of a little, tree-covered hill, and saw their pursuers, having given up the chase, return to their station. The Prince explained his wish to be put ashore with the statement that he would rather fight for his life than be taken prisoner, and he hoped God would never so afflict the King his father as to let him fall alive into the hands of his enemies.

On the little hill the Prince slept for three hours, and having re-embarked they rowed across the loch to a small island on its north shore—the south shore of Knoidart, that is—not far from the house of one of the Glengarry MacDonalds known as Scotus. Old Clanranald was then living there, who, it was hoped, would help them. Captain John went to look for him, and saw him a little way from Scotus's house. Clanranald hurried indoors, but John caught him by the coat-tail and held him. Clanranald turned, as if in surprise, and said, 'Oh, Mr. Mackinnon, is this you? I did not know you. How do you do? It is not easy to know people that come to visit us now.'

'Indeed,' said Captain John, 'it is hard nowadays to distinguish friends from foes. But I come as a friend, and have something to impart to you, if you will please to take a turn with me.'

In Scotus's garden, at the back of the house, they walked together, and to Clanranald's consternation he was told that Captain John had come, not merely with a message, but with orders for him. The Prince, who was not far away, commanded him to say into whose hands he could now confide himself. As Clanranald himself had not come out in the previous year, the Prince had no wish either to see him or to involve him in any personal danger. But Clanranald must name someone with whom Charles would be safe.

'What muckle devil has brought him to this country again?' demanded the unhappy chief, and talked wildly about the second destruction they could expect when troops came in again to raze and burn and rob. Captain John argued with him, spoke with severity about his duty and the Prince's utter dependence on friends and the help they could give him; but to no purpose.

'I tell you, Mr. Mackinnon,' said Clanranald, 'I know of no person into whose hands I can put him. But if my advice or opinion can be of any use, it is that you should directly return with him from whence you came, and land him speedily on the island of Rona.'

Rona, that narrow scrap of a rocky, pretty little island beyond Raasay, had already been visited and plundered, and Captain John was hardly exaggerating when he said that not a goat or a sheep could escape a search there, let alone a man. 'If this be the best advice or opinion you have to give,' he said, 'you had better keep it to yourself, for the following of it would be to throw the Prince directly into the hands of his enemies.'

He returned to the boat and repeated the conversation with Clanranald; to which the Prince, who had listened without any emotion, replied very easily, 'Well, Mr. Mackinnon, there is no help for it. We must do the best we can for ourselves.'

They returned to Mallaig, and with Captain John and old Mackinnon —whose age and infirmities seem to have been healed by a sense of loyalty and the urgency of his task—the Prince walked by night to a place called Cross in Morar, a mile or more south of the bridge over the Morar river. There was no bridge then, but the river could be forded, and at the north end of the ford Mackinnon asked their guide, whose name is unknown, if he would take a poor, sick young fellow on his back.—The Prince, it appears, was again disguised as an ailing servant.— 'The deil be on my back if he comes,' said the guide, 'or any fellow of a servant like him. But I'll take you on my back, Sir, if you please, and carry you safely through the ford.'

There is a temptation to pause at this point and consider the nature of society within the clan system. There is much to be said for a system which assures everyone within it of his intimate relationship with all his neighbours, their purpose and their interests, and excludes neither the half-wit nor the mischief-maker from a comforting sense of consanguinity. But the clan system was not without its disabilities, and if snobbery be accounted a disability, snobbery was certainly one of them. The girl at Elgol who refused to wash Lewie Caw's feet, and the gillie at the ford who would not carry him, were snobs to the marrow. Fraternity they knew, and they enjoyed their own sense of liberty; but equality was too ridiculous a notion even to consider. Enlist their loyalty, and the offer of a fortune could not dislodge them from it. But ask them to carry an ailing stranger, and a contemptuous refusal was their immediate reply. The reason, of course, is obvious. The clan system instilled in all its members a sense of dignity, a sense of individual worth, which had two equal but different voices: it could speak with heroic self-denial or fatuous self-importance without changing its accent.

The narrative must hurry, however, to keep pace with events.—The difficulty at the ford was solved when the old Mackinnon said, 'If the lad must wade, I'll wade along with him,' and the Prince, his identity unsuspected by the guide, crossed the river, which was running deep, with the stout-hearted old laird on his one side, and Captain John on the other.

At Cross in Morar they had hoped to find MacDonald of Morar; and find him they did, though not in his own house, which had been burnt. With his wife and children he was living in a bothy not far from its ruins, and most heartily he welcomed the Prince. A piece of cold salmon was warmed again for the travellers' meal, but there was no bread for them. When they had eaten they were taken to a nearby cave, where they slept. Morar had readily promised his service, and in the morning he went off to find the young Clanranald. But when he returned his manner had changed, he had become cool and reluctant. He had not, he said, been able to find Clanranald, and he himself could do nothing. It was pretty clear that someone—perhaps old Clanranald—had advised against helping the Prince; who spoke bitterly of those who had been glad to go with him when 'fortune smiled and I had pay to give', but now forsook him in his necessity. Captain John spoke angrily too, but Morar was unmoved.

Now, as never before, Charles showed the distress he felt. He was deeply hurt by the falling-away of those who had been his friends, and turning to Captain John exclaimed, 'I hope, Mr. Mackinnon, you will not desert me too, and leave me in the lurch, but that you'll do all for my preservation you can.'

The old Mackinnon thought it was he to whom the Prince had appealed, and with great emotion, the tears streaming down his cheeks, replied, 'I never will leave Your Royal Highness in the day of danger, but will, under God, do all I can for you, and go with you wherever you order me.'

The Prince thanked him heartily for such devotion, but said he had no intention of asking impossible service from so old a man. It was to Captain John he had spoken, and John, as zealous in loyalty as his chief, told him, 'With the help of God I will go through the wide world with Your Royal Highness, if you desire me.'

Charles now proposed to go to Borrodale again. It was not far away, and Aeneas MacDonald would be ready, he thought, to give what help he could. The Mackinnons did not know that part of the country, and Morar consented to let his son go as a guide; the boy had never seen the Prince before, and did not know who he was.

They reached Borrodale in the early morning—it was now the 10th July—and found Aeneas, like Morar, living in a bothy; for Captain Ferguson had burnt his house. He was asleep when Captain John went to the door, but came out with a blanket round him. He had heard nothing of the Prince, he said.

'What would you give for a sight of him?' asked Captain John.

'Time was,' replied Borrodale, rather enigmatically, 'that I would have given a hearty bottle to see him safe, but since I see you I expect to hear some news of him.'

'Well, then, I have brought him here,' said Captain John, 'and will commit him to your charge. I have done my duty. Do you yours.'

To his infinite credit Borrodale promptly replied, 'I am glad of it, and shall not fail to take care of him. I shall lodge him so secure that all the forces in Britain shall not find him.'

So hearty a reception must have done much to revive the Prince's spirit, and with the memory of the previous day's emotional scene fresh in his mind he may well have looked from Borrodale to the Mackinnons and felt that he still had friends on either side of him. There is a tradition in the Mackinnon family that before saying good-bye to the old chief he gave him a mysterious recipe for a strong cordial compounded largely of whisky—what would now be called a liqueur—and as he was fond of making small gifts at parting, and now had little left to give, there is no great difficulty in accepting the story. He had certainly much to be grateful for.

The old laird went back to Morar's bothy, where he was made prisoner next morning. Captain John found his way to the boat—the boatmen, presumably, had stayed with it somewhere near Mallaig—and got as far as Skye, but was taken in his own house that night.

At Borrodale the Prince lay hidden in a wood while John MacDonald—son of Aeneas and sometime a lieutenant in Clanranald's regiment—carried a message to his cousin, Alexander of Glenaladale; who was commanded to come and concert measures for His Royal Highness's safety. Glenaladale, who had been a major in Clanranald's regiment, was well known to the Prince.

When news arrived that old Mackinnon had been taken, it was thought prudent to remove the Prince to a cave in a high precipice—it was said to be inaccessible—some four miles to the east of the wood where he had lain. Borrodale and his son Ranald accompanied him, and on the 15th they were joined by Glenaladale who, though still suffering from the wounds he had got at Culloden, had left his wife and five small children to obey the Prince. Soon after his arrival a letter came from Borrodale's son-in-law, Angus MacEachine, to say it was rumoured already that His Royal Highness was in the neighbourhood, and it would be dangerous for him to stay longer in the cave. But he,

*A cave at Arisaig: home for a
fugitive?*

Angus, could offer him a safer refuge near Meoble on the Braes of Morar. Ranald MacDonald was sent to reconnoitre, but a day or two later, before his return, his brother John and Glenaladale were alarmed to see ships of war and small boats lying off the nearby coast, and soldiers ashore. Without waiting for Ranald to come back, the Prince set off to look for MacEachine's refuge at Meoble, about a mile north of the west end of Loch Eilt. With him went Glenaladale, Borrodale, and the latter's son John. On their way they met Angus MacEachine, who told them that young Clanranald was not far away, and he too offered a safe hiding-place. It was late in the day by then, so they went on to Meoble, and spent the night there.

Borrodale left them to look for food, and a report reached them that General Campbell with six men-of-war, all with troops aboard, had anchored in Loch Nevis. Two men went off to reconnoitre and report his movements, and Borrodale returned with the alarming news that Captain Caroline Scott had landed in the lower part of Arisaig. In effect, they were surrounded; there were camps established and sentries posted over all the wild upland country from the head of Loch Eil to the top of Loch Hourn. There was no chance now of their joining Clanranald, and their only hope was to break through or past the picket-line and reach some northern port such as Poolewe. For safety's sake the Prince's party was reduced, and now he was accompanied only by Glenaladale and his brother, and John the son of Borrodale. About midday they were on the top of a hill called Sgurr a' Mhuidhe, some 1,800 feet high and two or three miles west-by-north of what is now Glenfinnan Station. Glenaladale's brother went on to Glenfinnan, to seek news, and it was arranged to meet him again, at ten o'clock that night, on top of the great hill Sgurr nan Coireachan, over 3,000 feet high, that lies south-east of the head of Loch Morar.

The Prince and the two with him, marching a little east of north, were on Fraoch Beinn, north of Glenfinnan Station, by two o'clock in the afternoon. Then they saw cattle moving, and when Glenaladale

120

*Loch Shiel: view from the Monument*
*at Glenfinnan*

went forward to see what had disturbed them, he met some of his own clansmen shifting their beasts away from the advancing troops who, to the number of five or six hundred, had already reached the head of Loch Arkaig, and would quickly be athwart the route that the fugitives had meant to follow. Quickly their plans were altered, and while one of Glenaladale's clansmen went to fetch his brother from Glenfinnan, another set out to look for Donald Cameron of Glen Pean, who was thought to be in the neighbourhood and who might know if there was any chance of breaking through towards Fort Augustus.

The day was hot, and a woman of Glenaladale's clan stopped one of the driven cows to milk it, and brought the milk to her chieftain and the unknown young man who sat with him. The first messenger returned: he had not found Glenaladale's brother, but he brought news that a hundred militia-men from Argyll were already at the foot of the hill. There was no time to be lost—no time to wait for Cameron of Glen Pean—but off they went, about sunset, and before midnight, in a hollow between two hills, saw a man coming towards them; who was none other than Donald Cameron.

He knew something of the enemy's dispositions, and by paths forbidding even in daylight took them, by four in the morning, to a hill overlooking Loch Arkaig, from which they could see a militia camp not more than a mile away. But the hill on which they lay had already been searched, and there they remained all day, and happily were rejoined by Glenaladale's brother, who had followed them, it seems, by sheer instinct. At night they continued their march to the north, and came to Coire nan Gall, west of Loch Quoich, where they were uncomfortably aware, not only of the nearness of their enemies, but of hunger. They had nothing but a little oatmeal and a little butter. Most probably they had an iron griddle, but they dared not light a fire to make an oatcake.

From the head of Loch Eil to the top of Loch Hourn there were camps at intervals of half a mile, sentries were posted within call of

*Ben Nevis beyond Loch Eil*

each other, and regular patrols went out to see that the sentries were awake and watchful. When Robert Louis Stevenson, a hundred and forty years later, wrote in Bournemouth that superlative tale of Highland adventure, *Kidnapped*, he borrowed from the Prince's story the embarrassing affair of the tidal island, and there can be no doubt that his long and brilliantly exciting description of the flight through the heather, with Alan Breck and David Balfour in imminent, ever-present danger of capture, was directly inspired by the hardihood and ingenuity of Charles and his companions in circumstances of more prolonged and greater peril.

From their temporary security on the hill west of Loch Quoich Glenaladale's brother went off in search of food, and soon returned with two small cheeses and the news that a hundred redcoats were climbing the other side of the hill. The fugitives were well hidden and stayed where they were. The soldiers, though searching narrowly, failed to find them, and at eight o'clock in the evening the Prince and his friends turned north again, and from the top of another hill saw camp-fires directly in their path. They passed so close they could hear the soldiers talking, and on the summit of the next hill the scene was repeated. The fires of another camp burned in the darkness below. They made a little detour to the west, in dangerously steep country where the Prince, walking between Glenaladale and Cameron of Glen Pean, was saved by them from falling over a precipice when he slipped on a narrow, sloping path above it. In the early morning of the 21st they passed between two sentries in Glen Cosaidh, down which a stream that rises on the watershed between Loch Hourn and Loch Quoich tumbles into the latter.

They had now broken through the cordon, and marched on towards the head of Loch Hourn. They found shelter in a steep glen above Kinloch Hourn—great hills rising on either side—and rested all day in a hollow sheltered by old, long heather and young birches. All they had to eat was a little cheese dusted with oatmeal, but there was no lack of cold water, and for a relish to their meal they could watch forty soldiers

*The fugitives' path*

near the loch-shore below them. Before they set off again a reconnaissance discovered they had been lying within cannon-shot of two small
camps, but the night was intensely dark—though it was the night of the
full moon—and by sunrise they were in Glenshiel at a place about four
miles above Shiel Bridge, perhaps where the modern road crosses the
little stream called Mhalagain.

They crossed the Shiel and spent the day—again the weather was
distressingly hot—on the hillside north of the glen, not far from the
farm of Achnangairt. They were able to buy such simple provisions
as a stone of cheese and half a stone of butter from an honest man called
MacGrath; who in the evening sent his son to them with an additional
present of five Scots pints of goat's milk. But the Prince's hope of finding
a French ship at Poolewe was disappointed. A ship had called there,
and gone again. It was therefore decided to abandon what had been, at
best, a nebulous plan, and seek safety in a new direction. Donald
Cameron of Glen Pean could guide them no farther, and took his leave.
But a new guide came marvellously to replace him. Donald MacDonald,
a Glengarry man, was also on the run. Government soldiers had killed
his father the day before, and that morning had chased him into Glenshiel. He had served in the Prince's army, he seemed trustworthy, and he
could guide them to Glenmoriston where, it was now thought, there
was hope of finding temporary refuge. Their way lay eastward through
Glen Cluanie.

It was late at night when they started, and they had gone no more
than a quarter of a mile when Glenaladale discovered he had left his
purse behind; and in it was a more valuable purse that the Prince had
entrusted to him. He and young Borrodale went back to look for it,
and quickly found the outer purse. But the inner purse, with forty
louis d'or in it, had disappeared. Glenaladale suspected the boy who
had brought them goat's milk, and walked another mile to MacGrath's
house, where they found both boy and a very indignant father; with
whose help they got back the money, all 'but a trifle'. They returned,

*By dark Loch Hourn*

but by a different road, to where they had left the Prince, and found him waiting anxiously for them. An officer and two or three private soldiers had lately gone by, and the Prince had feared that Glenaladale would be intercepted. Had it not been for the missing purse, indeed, they might all have met the unknown officer head-on.

They walked till ten o'clock in the morning, and found shelter on a hillside somewhere above Loch Cluanie. It was another hot day, the midges were troublesome, and the Prince lay covered with heather to keep them off. They heard gunfire not far away, and turned north to climb a high hill between Loch Cluanie and Glen Affric. The weather changed, it rained heavily, and they spent the night in what is called an 'open cave' where they could neither sleep nor lie down. But a turn for the better in the Prince's fortune was not far off, and it was, it seems, the Glengarry man—the guide who had so providentially arrived—who was responsible for finding him a remarkable bodyguard.

The Glengarry man and Glenaladale's brother went off to meet their strange reinforcement, and a rendezvous was appointed at Corriegoe, north of Loch Cluanie. There the Prince met the Seven Men of Glenmoriston, who promptly became his devoted followers. They had all served in his army, and they are described as robbers. One, at least, had a wife and children whom he deserted to go with the Prince. They were a little band of self-sufficient and redoubtable fellows who had taken an oath of continuing hostility to Cumberland and his army, and decided to live as best they could—relying on strength and wit—in a lawless, ravished country. It may be thought indicative of the legendary quality of their service that the seven men were, in fact, eight. There were two MacDonalds, John and Alexander; three Chisholms, Alexander, Donald, and Hugh, who were brothers; Gregor MacGregor, Patrick Grant, and Hugh Macmillan—who, admittedly, joined them a little later. These broken men had it in their power to enrich themselves by £30,000, but in the dissolution of their society one thing had remained strangely intact, which was honour.

They swore allegiance in good Highland terms: 'That their backs should be to God and their faces to the Devil; that all the curses the Scriptures did pronounce might come upon them and all their posterity if they did not stand firm to help the Prince in his greatest dangers.' Charles had still much to fear, but not betrayal.

*Pistol, sword, and targe*

# XIII

THE character of the Prince's wandering now changes. His days were still arduous, he was often hungry, and such comfort as came his way was of a rude, barbaric sort; but danger had receded. Danger was still present, but no longer imminent, and as if to proclaim the improvement in his situation the Seven Men took him to a cave in which, under a roof of Cyclopean crags, a rocky ledge sheltered a bed of smooth gravel past which ran a little babbling stream; and in this romantic grotto, 'as comfortably lodged as if he had been in a royal palace', he lay safe for three days and recruited his strength. The Glenmoriston men were good foragers and brought in, to begin with, whisky and mutton, butter and cheese, but they could find no bread. They added a deer which they had shot and an ox they slaughtered; but still no bread.

After three days they removed to another shelter, another grotto as romantic in appearance and only two miles away, to avoid contact with the enemy. In the second cave they stayed four days, till the end of July, and then marched north to the Braes of Strathglass. There were, apparently, two reasons for this movement, the more immediate being the arrival of a certain Captain Campbell, called the Black Campbell, with a company of militia who encamped four miles away; and the other, the Prince's renewed interest in the possibility of going to Poolewe and finding a French ship there. In Strathglass they lodged in 'a sheally hut', a roughly made summer shieling, and two of the party were sent forward to Poolewe to get what news they could.

The main party followed more slowly into Glen Cannich, and on the 6th August climbed Beinn Acharain, north-west of Invercannich. This was the most northerly point of the Prince's wanderings, and nearby they found another 'sheally hut' to lie in. The messengers who had been sent to Poolewe returned with the news that only one French ship had been there, and though she had sailed again, two officers had been put ashore who were now said to be on their way to Lochiel's country, hoping to find the Prince there. It was therefore resolved to go south again, and look for the Frenchmen. They started by night, re-crossed the Cannich, and in the early morning reached Fasnakyle, where there is now a power station on the Affric.

At Fasnakyle, well sheltered in a wood, the Prince remained for three days while some of his party made a reconnaissance to see if the country was yet clear of troops. On the 12th a further advance was made to the Braes of Glenmoriston, east of Loch Cluanie, for it had been discovered that most of the militia had withdrawn to Fort Augustus. There were, however, still search-parties in Glengarry, and another night was spent in Glenmoriston while scouts again went forward and messengers were sent to Loch Arkaig to summon Cameron of Clunes; who, like his chief, had had his house burnt, and whose family had suffered great indignities.

The disputed area of the Highlands was still occupied by Government troops, but as a major operation the man-hunt was over. It had failed. Cumberland had gone from Fort Augustus on the 18th July, leaving Lord Albemarle in command, and on the 13th August the main body of Albemarle's army had marched away. There remained, in garrisons tactically situated, Lord Loudoun's regiment and seventeen companies of militia.

On the 14th the Prince and Glenaladale, with Glenaladale's brother, young John of Borrodale, and six of the Glenmoriston men—the other two having gone ahead to Loch Arkaig—marched to Glengarry, forded the swollen river, and under continuous heavy rain spent the night, without shelter of any sort, on the side of a hill a mile beyond it. In the morning it was still raining, and they had nothing to eat. But they went on as far as Achnasaul at the east end of Loch Arkaig, where they spent a wretched day in some sort of hut or bothy where it seemed to rain as heavily indoors as out. It was there the messengers had been instructed to return, and it was necessary to wait for them because none of the Prince's party knew that corner of the country. They were growing desperate with hunger, for in that robbed and ravished land they could find nothing to eat—no inhabitants indeed, for all seemed to have fled—when the messengers returned with instruction from Cameron of Clunes. They were to go to a wood two miles away, where he would meet them in the morning. They found good shelter there, and on the way one of the Glenmoriston men shot a fine stag and saved them from starvation. MacDonald of Glengarry joined them there, in time to share the first good meal they had had for several days.

Clunes duly came to meet them, and another messenger was despatched to summon Lochiel. He did not come himself, but sent his brother Dr. Cameron—who was later hanged—and the Rev. John Cameron, sometime Presbyterian chaplain at Fort William; and the Rev. John later recorded his delightful memory of the picture that the Prince presented.

It was still not safe to move freely about the country, and Dr. Cameron and the Rev. John crossed the river with some care, and approached with caution the hut on the north shore of Loch Arkaig where the Prince had lain. He was not there. Another of the Camerons, of Achnasaul, had joined him, and they were on the hill above. But when the Prince heard that visitors had arrived, he came down to the loch, and as the Rev. John first saw him he was 'bare-footed, had an old black kilt coat on, philabeg and waistcoat, a dirty shirt and a long red beard, a gun in his hand, a pistol and dirk by his side. He was very cheerful and in good health, and in my opinion fatter than when he was in Inverness.'

That is the picture of a man who, having been brought up in the tame luxury of an exiled court, had learnt how to live like an outlaw, a partisan, a folk-hero; and perhaps a better portrait than pretty pictures of him in Highland finery. The red beard, the dirty shirt, and the musket under his arm are necessary correctives of popular artistic fiction.

They moved towards Achnacarry, Lochiel's blackened house, and there, it is probable, met the two French officers they had been looking for; whose despatches were of no interest or importance. It is uncertain

133

what happened next. Glenaladale's brother and that good young man, Borrodale's son, may have gone to the west coast to watch for ships. The French officers disappeared. Dr. Cameron and Cameron of Clunes and Lochgarry went about their own business. There was an alarm when a detachment of Loudoun's regiment was reported near at hand. The Prince and Glenaladale and others retired to the Braes of Glen Kingie, between Loch Arkaig and Loch Quoich, and the Prince slept in his plaid, battered by hail as well as rain. They returned to Achnacarry, and the brave men of Glenmoriston—all but Patrick Grant—were dismissed. They had served their turn.

Lochgarry and Dr. Cameron came again, with news from Lochiel that the Prince would be safe where he himself was in hiding. At that the Prince was well pleased, and set out on a long march to Badenoch, east of the Great Glen. Before he crossed the Lochy—where now the Caledonian Canal leads into Loch Lochy—he said good-bye to Patrick Grant, and gave him twenty-four guineas to be divided among the men of Glenmoriston. They, who spoke nothing but Gaelic, had had some pretty contentions with him—Glenaladale was their interpreter—and would tell him when to eat, if they had anything to eat, or rest if they thought it necessary. On one occasion when he wanted to move before they thought it safe, they threatened to tie him rather than comply with him. 'Kings and princes must be ruled by their privy council,' said Charles, 'but I believe there is not in all the world a more absolute privy council than what I have at present.' That was the only time they positively differed with him, and later, says Patrick Grant, 'we were very sorry for it.'

Glenaladale said good-bye to the Prince when Lochgarry and Dr. Cameron took charge of him; he had been in attendance for rather more than six weeks, and accompanied Charles through the most desperate passages of his flight. Three times wounded at Culloden, his estate ruined, his loyalty remained unflawed, and with an invincible spirit went a capacity of physical endurance that was truly remarkable;

for one of his wounds, when he joined the Prince, was only partially healed. He lived until January, 1761, and died unexpectedly in Moidart in his forty-ninth year.

On the 30th August the Prince met Lochiel by Loch Ericht, on the south-eastern slope of Ben Alder, a great hill that rises to more than 3,700 feet about twenty-five miles east of Fort William. It was a joyful occasion, for the Prince's mood was gay and Lochiel or those with him had prepared what must have seemed, after lean days in the heather, a state banquet. There was mutton and 'an anker of whisky of twenty Scots pints', well-cured beef sausages, butter and cheese and a bacon-ham. The hut in which they ate was small and smoky, but the Prince's appetite was good. He took a hearty dram when he went in, and called for a good many more to drink the health of so many friends. He was given a silver spoon, and ate heartily from a large sauce-pan of minced collops. 'Now, gentlemen, I live like a prince,' he said. He asked Lochiel, a little enviously, if he had been accustomed to living so richly, and Lochiel, still lame from his wounds, admitted that Cluny had looked after him very well.

Cluny himself—Ewen MacPherson, chief of the clan—had gone to Achnacarry to look for the Prince, but returned on the 1st September, and after two or three days they moved a couple of miles higher up the hill to 'a romantic comical habitation' known as Cluny's Cage. The site of this is uncertain. The Ordnance Survey marks it confidently, but it may well have been on a higher slope. It was concealed by a grove of holly, it afforded wide views, and was constructed, against the steepness of the ground, on two floors, and was roofed with turf. Against a great slab of grey rock behind it the smoke from its chimney was invisible, and with a fire to warm them six or seven people could find room to play cards and cook another meal.

There, for a week, the Prince lived in such comfort as he had not known for a long time; having for company and attendance Lochiel, Cluny, Lochgarry, and Dr. Cameron; Allan Cameron, who was

135

Lochiel's chief servant, and four of Cluny's servants. Cluny's brother-in-law, MacPherson of Breakachie, was sent to find Colonel John Roy Stewart, a friend of the Prince's, and enquire about shipping. Before he returned they heard there were French ships in Loch nan Uamh, and at one o'clock in the morning of the 13th set off on a last journey, and spent the next day in a hut lower down the hill. There they were joined by Breakachie and John Roy, who had not been told of the Prince's presence. Charles, in holiday spirits, lay down completely hidden in a plaid, and surprised John Roy by suddenly peeping out: the Colonel fainted and fell into a puddle at the door.

They marched north, between Ben Alder and Loch Ericht, then west through the Ben Alder Forest and past the south end of Loch Laggan towards Glen Roy. They moved by night, lay hidden and rested by day. They crossed Glen Roy, and the river Lochy by moonlight in a crazily leaking boat, and came to Achnacarry. Another day there, and by night along Loch Arkaig. Cluny and Dr. Cameron had gone ahead to provide food, and a cow was killed and bannocks baked for a last meal before the last day's march to Borrodale.

It was the 19th September when, in the very place where he had landed fourteen months before, the Prince and Lochiel with many followers went aboard the ship *L'Heureux*, which before midnight weighed anchor and set sail for France.

But Cluny remained in Scotland. He was, said the Prince, 'the only person in whom he could repose the greatest confidence', and his task now was to make preparation for Charles's return. So Cluny went back to his cage, and for eight years waited, without reward, for the Prince to come into his own again.

*The Beach at Loch nan Uamh*

*The Town of Mallaig*

# XIV

TWENTY-SEVEN years later, in 1773, Dr. Johnson astonished his London friends by setting out on a tour of the Scottish Highlands and Islands in company with his dissolute young friend James Boswell. They rode to the west, crossed over to Skye, and from Skye to Raasay. Their pilot on the latter voyage was Malcolm MacLeod: the Captain Malcolm who in 1746 had walked with the Prince from Portree to Elgol. Boswell describes him: 'He was now sixty-two years of age, quite the Highland gentleman; of a stout well-made person, well-proportioned; a manly countenance browned with the weather, but a ruddiness in his cheeks, a good way up which his rough beard extended; a quick lively eye, not fierce in his look, but firm and good-humoured. He had a pair of brogues, tartan hose which came up only near to his knees and left them bare, a purple kilt, a black waistcoat, a short cloth green coat with gold cord, a large blue bonnet with a gold-thread button. I never saw a figure that was so perfectly a representative of a Highland gentleman. I wished much to have a picture of him just as he was. I found him frank and *polite*, in the true sense of the word.'

On the crossing to Raasay Captain Malcolm started that rousing song, *Tha tighinn fodham éiridh*, the four boatmen and the Rev. Mr. MacQueen, who went with them, joining in; and in the course of the next day or two he told Boswell several anecdotes about his share in the great adventure. He spoke of the time when he and the Prince, and his cousins young Rona and Murdoch, were lying in the miserable hut on Raasay, and were alarmed by the approach of the suspect pedlar. The MacLeods had thought it best to shoot him, the Prince had objected to taking the life of a man who might be innocent, and Mackenzie, one of their boatmen, had replied, in Gaelic, 'Well, well, no matter. He must be shot. You are the King, but we are the Parliament.' His reply being translated, said Malcolm, the Prince had laughed 'loud and heartily', in despite of danger—and the pedlar had saved his life by taking another path.

Mackenzie the boatman was still alive, and Boswell saw and spoke to him. He had suffered some injury to a leg while dancing. So serious an injury, indeed, that the leg had had to be amputated. But he had replaced it with a wooden one, and was still active. He had sound democratic principles, and had not changed his opinion that kings should be controlled by their parliaments: 'Where,' he said, 'there are many voices against one.'

Malcolm had been taken prisoner and sent to London to stand his trial. For want of evidence he was released, and Flora MacDonald, also a prisoner, was set free about the same time, and by Lady Primrose provided with a post-chaise to take her to Edinburgh. She could, she was told, choose any one of her friends as her companion; and she chose Malcolm. 'So I,' said he, 'went to London to be hanged, and came down in a chaise with Miss Flora MacDonald.'

The island itself had recovered from the dreadful punishment it had suffered, and young Rona, who had succeeded his father and become the laird—young Rona was now Raasay—had rebuilt his house in a substantial way, and entertained his visitors as handsomely as could be desired. Boswell, who appreciated a good table, describes their reception with manifest pleasure: 'We found here coffee and tea in genteel order upon the table, as it was past six when we arrived: diet loaf, marmalade of oranges, currant jelly; some elegantly bound books on a large table, in short, all the marks of improved life. We had a dram of excellent brandy, according to the Highland custom, filled round. They call it a *scalck*. On a sideboard was served up directly, for us who had come off the sea, mutton-chops and tarts, with porter, claret, mountain, and punch. Then we took coffee and tea. In a little, a fiddler appeared, and a little ball began. Raasay himself danced with as much vigour and spirit as any man.'

Raasay had fathered a family of three boys and ten girls, and Boswell, with the gravity of one who was himself not long married, thought he might find it difficult to get husbands for so many daughters; but his fears were groundless, and they all married well. For a last sight of

Captain Malcolm it is necessary to envisage a curious gathering at the top of Dun Cann, the lopped-off cone of a hill that dominates the island. Malcolm and Boswell, with several others, had gone out shooting, and climbed the hill, 'where we sat down, eat cold mutton and bread and cheese and drank brandy and punch. Then we had a Highland song from Malcolm; then we danced a reel to which he and Donald Macqueen sang.'—The picture of Captain Malcolm, at the age of sixty-two, singing heartily on the top of Dun Cann, is as pretty a conclusion to adventure as one could wish for.

Not all his fellow Jacobites were so fortunate, but Neil MacEachain, the quiet and modest schoolmaster whom some took for Miss Mac-Donald's servant, was so much the master of events that he lived to write with vivid amusement about them, and outraged probability by becoming the father of a duke. MacEachain, who had evaded capture, managed to get to France with the Prince, and there, assuming his proper patronymic of MacDonald, joined Ogilvy's Scots regiment. In the course of time he retired on pension, married a talkative, quick-tempered French girl with whom he was not always happy, and begot four children of whom two, a boy and a girl, survived their infancy. The boy, Etienne MacDonald, became a soldier, supported the revolution, distinguished himself at Jemappes, and eventually was made a Marshal of France and Duke of Taranto.

Ned Burke also escaped capture, but after leaving the Prince suffered terrible privations for many weeks in the island of his birth, North Uist. He finally escaped to the mainland, where he was sheltered by Alexander MacLeod, sometime the Prince's aide-de-camp. When it became permissible to do so, he returned to Edinburgh and his old occupation at one end of a sedan-chair. In 1747 he appeared 'both stout and sturdy' despite the hardships he had suffered, and was then 'not much above forty years of age.' But he died in 1751. Always poor and quite illiterate, he still, as his epitaph has it, 'preferred a good conscience to thirty thousand pounds.'

He and old Donald MacLeod, the pilot of the eight-oared boat, met in Edinburgh after Donald's release from the prison-hulks at Tilbury, and argued warmly about their memories of the adventure. In London Donald had been given, by an admirer, a very handsome silver snuff-box with the boat, and Donald at the helm, modelled on the lid. Round the edge was inscribed *Olim haec meminisse juvabit*, and on the bottom 'Donald MacLeod of Gualtergill, in the Isle of Skye, the faithful Palinurus'. But when he returned to Edinburgh he was quite penniless, and but for Bishop Forbes might have been unable to reach Skye, where his wife and family were. The Bishop collected £10 for him, being a pound a week for the ten weeks he had served the Prince, and Donald went home; where he died, at the age of seventy-two, in 1749.

The chief of the Mackinnons, after being taken in MacDonald of Morar's bothy, was eventually sent to the abominable prison-hulks at Tilbury, where Donald of Gualtergill lay and so many died of ill-treatment and inanition. On Donald's testimony the old laird—who was not nearly so old as Donald himself—endured hardship better than most of the younger men, and during what was evidently an epidemic of some sort he was 'only about eight days in such a way that he needed one to help him up in the morning.' He was released in the summer of 1747, and lived, in high spirits and with the most agreeable eccentricity, until 1756, when Bishop Forbes recorded his death with great felicity:

'*May 7th*, 1756.—Died at his house of Kilmane in the Isle of Sky, John MacKinnon of that Ilk, *i.e.*, the old Laird of MacKinnon, in the 75th year of his age, leaving issue two sons and a daughter, Charles, Lachlan, and Margaret, all born after the 71st year of his age. He used to say he hoped God would not take him off the earth but on the field of battle when fighting for his king and country. He frequently retired to the cave in which the Prince and he himself and his lady dined just before the Prince's leaving Sky in his sculking, and there he would have entertained himself with laying down a plan for the restoration, and with the execution thereof in theory, and then came home extremely well pleased.'

Captain John Mackinnon, after being made prisoner at Elgol, was put aboard Captain Ferguson's ship *Furness*, and there was so fortunate as to find General Campbell of Mamore, that courteous and good-hearted man. The General, it is evident, took a liking to Captain John, gave him wine, and on one occasion not only drank to him but made the abominable Ferguson do the same. Captain John was among those sent to Tilbury, and his later years were unhappy. By 1761 he was 'afflicted with a lameness from the tops of his thighs down', and had been in hospital in Edinburgh for several months. He had no chance of a cure, it was decided, unless he went to Bath; but that he could not afford to do. The indefatigable Bishop Forbes raised a subscription, amounting to £18 8s. od., and Captain John was carried south for further, unavailing treatment. He died in Bath, and was buried there, in May, 1762, at the age of forty-eight.

Captain Donald Roy MacDonald, wounded in the foot at Culloden, who avoided capture, lived out his life as a farmer and schoolmaster in North Uist. A country schoolmaster in Skye had given him a classical education good enough to let him amuse himself, while on the run, by writing Latin odes to his lame foot and the disastrous battle; and he repaid the debt by teaching his neighbours' sons in the Long Island.

Of the Glenmoriston men the most articulate was Patrick Grant, though John MacDonald was their leader. It was Grant who told Bishop Forbes, with seemly pride, that all eight of them had been 'bred to the military discipline' in various independent Highland companies as well as in the Prince's army; and that being so, their behaviour takes on a little more consequence. When they pledged themselves to continue a private war against Cumberland, they knew what they were doing, and in attack on a military convoy near Glenelg they showed a nice tactical appreciation of ground. Shortly before attaching themselves to the Prince, they had captured and beheaded a notorious spy and informer —another Grant—and against their military background that act of savage justice may be extenuated as the decision of a drum-head court-martial. They should be respected as conscious partisans, and it is agreeable to learn that the character of Patrick Grant was such as to gain the admiration of some friends who, after the indemnity, commissioned a portrait of him.

In his several talks with the Bishop his most unexpected revelation was that John MacDonald, their leader, was in fact a Campbell who had found it advantageous to change his name. Patrick, as a pressed man, served briefly in a North American campaign against the French, in or about 1759, but by some unrevealed, old-soldierly device got quickly home again and was given a Chelsea pension. He and John MacDonald were still living in Glenmoriston, though in poor circumstances, in 1763. Alexander MacDonald and Alexander Chisholm died in 1751, and of the other four nothing is known.

The most famous of the Prince's associates, Flora MacDonald, lived a life that was both uncommonly eventful and strictly conventional. After her arrest she was compelled to remain for three weeks aboard the *Furness*, but was then transferred to the *Eltham* whose Captain Smith, an Englishman, allowed her, with General Campbell's approval, to go ashore near Armadale to supply herself with a maid and some clothes. In the *Eltham* and in the *Bridgewater*, Captain Knowles, in which she was confined for some weeks at the port of Leith, she was treated not merely with humanity but with consideration and respect; and when, in November, she returned to the *Eltham* to go to London, a great crowd cheered as the ship sailed. For a little while she was held in the Tower, but her subsequent imprisonment, until the Act of Indemnity in July, 1747, was in the house of a Government messenger where she was allowed much freedom and paid six and eightpence a day for her board. Before she returned to Scotland, in the chaise provided by Lady Primrose with Malcolm MacLeod to escort her, Lady Primrose had collected a fund of fifteen hundred guineas for her: a handsome testimonial and a curious comment on the English character.

Flora was sensible enough to take some pleasure from her reception in Edinburgh, and was in no great hurry to return to Skye. But if she accepted flattery she did not let it turn her head, and at Armadale, in November, 1750, she married Allan MacDonald, son of the Prince's most generous of hosts, good Kingsburgh and his lady. She and Allan lived at Flodigarry, far to the north on the east coast of the long peninsula of Trotternish, with the view before them of the great hills of Torridon, and in the next sixteen years she did her duty to her husband by bearing ten children. Old Kingsburgh died in 1772, at the age of eighty-three, and Allan and Flora then removed to the house where the Prince, as Betty Burke, had lain.

There, in the year after old Kingsburgh's death, they received their distinguished visitor Dr. Johnson and his young friend Boswell. Allan MacDonald, says Boswell, 'had his tartan plaid thrown about him, a large blue bonnet with a knot of black ribbon like a cockade, a brown short coat of a kind of duffle, a tartan vest with gold buttons and gold buttonholes, a bluish filibeg, and tartan hose. He had jet-black hair tied behind and with screwed ringlets on each side, and was a large stately man, with a steady sensible countenance.

'There was a comfortable parlour with a good fire, and a dram of admirable Holland's gin went round. By and by supper came, when there appeared his spouse, the celebrated Miss Flora. She was a little woman, of a mild and genteel appearance, mighty soft and well-bred. To see Mr. Samuel Johnson salute Miss Flora MacDonald was a wonderful romantic scene to me.'

Johnson lay in the bed, with tartan curtains, where the Prince had slept, and Boswell, though he shared in the drinking of three bowls of punch after supper, was grieved 'to recollect that Kingsburgh had fallen sorely back in his affairs, was under a load of debt, and intended to go to America.' No complaint or sign of hardship interrupted hospitality, but in 1774 Kingsburgh and his wife and family had to emigrate. The ship in which they sailed was attacked by a French privateer, and in the action Flora was wounded in the arm. The popular story that she remained on deck to encourage the gunners is probably untrue, but there may well have been need for bandages and a strong-minded nurse.

In North Carolina Kingsburgh bought land, and in the American War of Independence served on the side of the British Government. Flora came home in 1779, and lived in South Uist till her husband returned five years later. They went back to the old house of Kingsburgh, and in 1790, at the age of sixty-eight, Flora died and was buried at Kilmuir, a couple of miles north of Monkstadt. She was a woman, wrote Johnson, 'of middle stature, soft features, gentle manners, and elegant presence'; and as he foretold she left a name that has been 'mentioned in history', and where 'courage and fidelity be virtues, mentioned with honour.'

Of the latter days of the Prince himself one can write only with sorrow, for, as if defeat had drained the sole purpose of his life, its last remnant was without form and void. In his renewed exile he did not, however, admit defeat easily. In France he was received with popular enthusiasm, but the King was coldly discreet. Charles pleaded for an army of 20,000 men to save the realm of Scotland, and the French king snubbed him with the offer of a pension. His father, the old Pretender, had lost heart and hope; his brother, the Duke of York, retired from political or family life to the shelter of a cardinal's hat. Charles was driven into isolation. His stubborn refusal to accept either defeat or a pension exasperated Louis XV, and Charles was arrested and expelled from France. He became friendly, in succession, with several distinguished ladies, but his relations with them remain obscure. It seems certain that politics and his dynastic ambition were still his dominating interest.

The Hanoverian government was implacably hostile, but there was a revival of Jacobite sympathy in England, and in 1750 Charles received

*The Monument at Glenfinnan*

a large sum of money from an unknown source, and daringly appeared in London. A Dr. King, a prominent Jacobite, met him at Lady Primrose's house in Essex Street, and later recorded: 'If I was surprised to find him there, I was still more astonished when he acquainted me with the motives which had induced him to hazard a journey to England at this juncture. The impatience of his friends who were in exile had formed a scheme which was impracticable, but although it had been as feasible as they had represented it to him, yet no preparation had been made, nor was anything ready to carry it into execution. He was soon convinced that he had been deceived; and, therefore, after a stay in London of five days only, he returned to the place from whence he came.'

He went to see Frederick the Great in Berlin, who was not unsympathetic but gave no help. A *coup de main* was discussed, and the Prince's agent in Antwerp was commanded to procure 26,000 muskets. The conspirators involved in the Elibank plot proposed to kidnap the Hanoverian royal family—Charles insisted that no harm must befall them—but the plot was betrayed and came to nothing.

Charles formed an association with Clementina Walkinshaw, who had nursed him through an illness after the battle of Falkirk; and their relationship had unhappy consequences. It was about this time that Charles started drinking heavily. His life grew increasingly wretched, again he was a wanderer—no longer pursued by redcoats, but beset by spies and informers—and as despair soured his temper, so progressively he alienated old friends.

In December, 1765, Charles went back to Rome to see his dying father, but arrived too late. The Vatican declined to recognise him as Charles III, but now, for some time, he lived a regular and sober life, moving in Roman society as Count Albany. In 1772 he married, by French persuasion, the young Princess Louise of Stolberg. The marriage was ill advised, and again he took to drink, Louise to adultery with the rich Italian dramatist, Count Vittorio Alfieri. Charles fell ill, succumbed to melancholia, and lived in drab loneliness in Florence. Charlotte, his

148

daughter by Clementina Walkinshaw, joined him in 1784, and brought him a little happiness. But his brain was much disturbed, he could not bear to be reminded of the bloodshed he had seen in Scotland. Music and Charlotte could still give him pleasure, but his will to live had failed, and in January, 1788, a paralytic stroke was the herald of death that came a few hours later. Charlotte did not long survive him.

His life—all of it that amounted to anything—was lived in Scotland between the 25th July, 1745, and the 19th September, 1746—and what is one to say of that desperate, heart-breaking, long year?

As a political action his attempt to regain the throne had no consequence but total and disastrous failure, and judiciously it can be seen as an impossible attempt to put back the clock of history. For an assault on the monarchy accepted, however grudgingly, by England and most of Scotland he relied on the support of some—not all, be it noted, but only some—of the Highland clans; and the society they preserved was already an anachronism. There was much to admire in the clan system, but it possessed two fatal defects: the loyalties inherent in it made co-operation on a general scale impossible, and it was a closed society that prohibited change. In Clan Donald and the Camerons and their hardy neighbours reposed many virtues, but—as Duncan Forbes of Culloden so clearly saw—they possessed no weapons for an assault, in the 18th century, on the established strength of England. The drinking Jacobites, who toasted the King over the Water but declined to fight for him, elicit no admiration, but in the sobriety of morning they could tell the time of day.

Political success, however, is not the only standard by which to judge behaviour, and in another assessment Charles Edward Stuart, and those who rallied to his cause, won the world's ultimate reward. The reward, that is, of the sort of immortality which the world gives to stories of romantic endeavour supported by that greatness of spirit of which humanity is sometimes capable.

The worth of such a reward is, of course, debatable. That Bonnie

Prince Charlie brought sorrow and ruin to the Highlands is incontestable; and yet, by a not uncommon paradox, he enriched them beyond measure by a story that lives, and probably will, among the great stories of the world.

That he, throughout the long months of his flight, became a man of the proper sort to inspire such a story—a man whose girth of being and brightness of spirit were sufficient to inspire devotion—has been made clear by the tale of his wanderings. But the devotion he inspired is the greater part of the story, and the blackened years of Highland desolation are still lighted by the memory of such men and women as Donald MacLeod and Malcolm MacLeod, as MacEachain and Donald Roy and the good Mackinnons, as humble Ned Burke and the gallant Irishmen O'Sullivan and O'Neil, as the Seven Men of Glenmoriston, as Glenaladale, as Kingsburgh and his lady, and Flora MacDonald in her grave and steadfast beauty.

Charles was the candle who lighted the bonfire, but they were the timber that filled a dark sky with their splendid ardour.

*Culloden Moor*

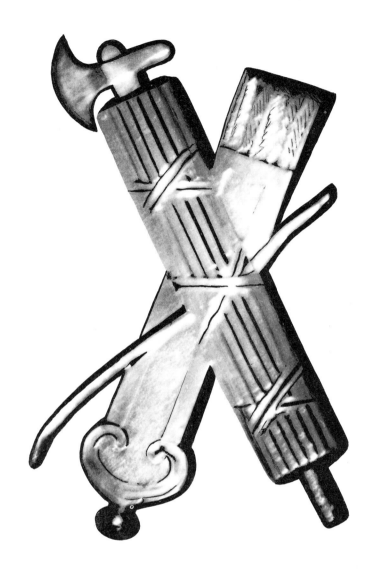

# A NOTE ON SOURCES

*The Lyon in Mourning*, published in three volumes by the Scottish History Society in 1895, 'is a collection of Journals, Narratives, and Memoranda relating to the life of Prince Charles Edward Stuart at and subsequent to the Jacobite Rebellion of 1745. The formation of this collection was to a great extent the life-work of the Rev. Robert Forbes, M.A., Bishop of Ross and Caithness.'

Born in Aberdeenshire in 1708, and a graduate of the Marischal College of Aberdeen, the Bishop was an ardent Jacobite. Arrested while on his way to join the Prince, he was imprisoned at first in Stirling, then in Edinburgh Castle. There he met many who had shared in the great adventure, listened to the tales they told, and resolved to commit to writing as many first-hand narratives as he could collect. Despite his politics he was scrupulous in his search for facts, reverent of dates, names, and places, and loved the truth 'let who will be either justified or condemned by it.'

The story, told here, is drawn almost entirely from *The Lyon in Mourning*, but the Bishop's great collection is not an orderly assemblage, and I am vastly indebted to the *Itinerary* compiled from those rich volumes by Walter Biggar Blaikie and published in 1897.

# NOTES ON THE PHOTOGRAPHS

## by Don Kelly

The first thing about taking pictures in Scotland is that the landscape won't stand still . . . it changes size, shape, and mood, all in the few seconds it takes to set up your camera—what you thought you saw only minutes before is now all magically different and rearranged in your viewfinder.

There are two ways of solving the problem—and both work. Since your subject is always on the move, you can do the opposite. You can stand still and wait for *it*—ready for that fleeting shift of light, or mist, or cloud, that transforms the view before you into the picture you wanted—or something even better. This can be exciting and challenging—*and frustrating*! Or you can move and shift *with* the subject—and this means mentally and emotionally as well as physically . . . camera at the ready for instant action—hand held and off the tripod. There is an element of the hunt in both methods—and the quarry *is* elusive.

The moody, deceivingly luminous light levels prevalent in the Highlands of Scotland can be very misleading. The visual judgment of the contrast range can deceive the human eye into assuming a much lower range than actually exists. The correct exposure-development combination becomes very important if the exact effect is not to be ruined by an excessive contrast between the sky and the land or water areas.

The human eye adjusts more readily to the separate subtle gradations in light values than does any negative material. So many of the subjects in the Highlands are made up of two large main masses—the moody area of the skies, with their dramatic rolling tones of grey can be a lot lighter than you think, and the dark land areas full of subtle low key tones can be a lot darker than you think.

The use of filters is not the answer, except perhaps when the sky is broken and showing patches of blue. Filters have ruined more good photographs than they have made . . . their heavy-handed use can obliterate the subtle luminous tones in the large dark areas in the kind of subject we are discussing.

Nor is the technique of taking separate meter readings of the main areas and then averaging them out the answer. This use of the meter is, after all, a compromise with the subject, and much of the delicate tone structure in *both* areas can be lost.

My personal answer has been the use of exposure-development combinations in the manipulation of tonal values in the negative towards a pre-visualised effect in the print. With certain modifications this approach is based upon the classic rule—'expose for the shadows and develop for the lights'—and demands a more than passing familiarity with your materials . . . films, developers, and papers.

The exposure meter is used in two capacities—first, to determine the correct exposure for the darkest part of the scene in which you want to see detail. This exposure can be calculated on most reflected light meters by an adjustment towards a two stop decrease in the exposure indicated. (Or the exposure index could be set on the meter to compensate, and the reading taken directly.) This is the exposure that ensures adequate detail in the important shadow areas . . .

Then measure the *highest* important light value in the scene. This determines the development time—less development is indicated when the range between important shadow detail and important highlight detail is long—more development when the range is short . . . the amount of over or under-development depending upon the amount of expansion or contraction of the tonal range you wish to get into your negative . . . aimed towards the final effect you want to see in the print.

The complications of this approach are only apparent, in the explanation—and rapidly become second nature and automatic in practice.★

Most of the pictures in this book were taken during the last two weeks in October . . . The best time of day was found to be the early morning, when the winds were moving the clouds at different levels—often in different directions—thinning them out in places and allowing sunlight to filter through

★ Complete details of the techniques involved can be found brilliantly and lucidly expounded in the writings and work of Ansel Adams.

in shafts. All too often at this time of the year the clouds congeal later in the day into a solid unbroken grey—making photography impossible. Every once in a while the clouds will break up again late in the afternoon, and the sky on the west coast will blaze into some of the most spectacular sunsets to be found anywhere in the world. Mostly—it's a matter of luck . . .

Of course there are many sunny days in the Highlands. Fortunately perhaps for most people who visit Scotland, they coincide with the summer holiday season. In many ways, it is more difficult to get good pictures when conditions seem perfect—all too often the result is merely an obvious and tritely 'pretty' picture. The Highlands of Scotland are worthy of a deeper interpretation, and are capable of rewarding observation, patience, thought, and effort with some deeply profound photographic experiences.

The following technical information relating to the pictures in this book is offered to those kind enough to have looked at them and curious enough to want to know a little more about how they were taken . . .

The camera used for most of the pictures was a $2\frac{1}{4}''$ square Bronica Single-lens Reflex, with a $4'' \times 5''$ Speed Graphic and a $35$ mm. Nikon Single-lens Reflex.

The black-and-white films used were mostly Kodak Plus X and Tri-X, and they were developed in Acufine and Acutol. The original prints were enlarged on to Kodak Press F paper and developed in D.163.

Some deviations were made from the manufacturers' exposure and development recommendations—generally favouring full to over exposure and under-development . . .

The colour pictures were taken on Kodak Ektachrome.

# BLACK AND WHITE ILLUSTRATIONS

| Page | Camera | Lens | Stop F. Number | Shutter Speed | Film and Developer | Time + or − Normal |
|---|---|---|---|---|---|---|
| 6 | Bronica | 50 | 11 | 1/125 | Plus X Acutol | − Normal |
| 9 | Bronica | 135 + 1 extension | 16 | 1/8 | Plus X Acutol | + Normal |
| 11 | Bronica | 50 | 11 | 1/125 | Plus X Acutol | − Normal |
| 13 | Bronica | 50 | 11 | 1/60 | Plus X Acutol | − Normal |
| 15 | Bronica | 50 | 11 | 1/250 | Plus X Acutol | − Normal |
| 17 | Bronica | 50 | 11 | 1/125 | Plus X Acutol | − Normal |
| 19 | Bronica | 50 | 8 | 1/125 | Plus X Acutol | − Normal |
| 21 | Bronica | 135 | 11 | 1/250 | Tri-X Acufine | Normal |
| 23 | Bronica | 135 | 8 | 1/60 | Plus X Acutol | − Normal |
| 27 | Nikon | 105 | 11 | 1/125 | Plus X Acutol | Normal |
| 29 | Nikon | 50 | 8 | 1/125 | Plus X Acutol | − Normal |
| 32 | Nikon | 50 | 11 | 1/250 | Tri-X Acufine | + Normal |
| 34 | Nikon | 135 | 16 | 1/250 | Tri-X Acufine | + Normal |
| 36 | Nikon | 135 | 11 | 1/500 | Tri-X Acufine | + Normal |
| 39 | Nikon | 50 | 8 | 1/125 | Tri-X Acufine | + Normal |
| 41 | Nikon | 135 | 8 | 1/125 | Plus X Acutol | − Normal |
| 45 | Nikon | 50 | 16 | 1/250 | Tri-X Acufine | + Normal |

| Page | Camera | Lens | Stop F. Number | Shutter Speed | Film and Developer | Time + or − Normal |
|------|--------|------|----------------|---------------|--------------------|--------------------|
| 47 | Nikon | 50 | 16 | 1/60 | Plus X Acutol | −Normal |
| 49 | Nikon | 105 | 11 | 1/250 | Plus X Acutol | Normal |
| 57 | Bronica | 50 | 16 | 1/250 | Tri-X Acufine | Normal |
| 59 | Bronica | 50 | 4 | 1/125 | Plus X Acutol | −Normal |
| 73 | Nikon | 105 | 4 | 1/500 | Plus X Acutol | −Normal |
| 76 | Bronica | 50 | 11 | 1/250 | Plus X Acufine | −Normal |
| 79 | Bronica | 50 | 16 | 1/4 | Plus X Acutol | −Normal |
| 80 | Bronica | 135 | 11 | 1/500 | Tri-X Acufine | Normal |
| 91 | Bronica | 135 1 extension tube | 16 | 1/4 | Plus X Acutol | +Normal |
| 94 | Bronica | 50 | 11 | 1/30 | Plus X Acutol | −Normal |
| 97 | Bronica | 135+ extension tube | 16 | 1/2 | Plus X Acutol | +Normal |
| 105 | Bronica | 135 | 22 | 1/4 | Plus X Acutol | −Normal |
| 111 | Bronica | 50 | 8 | 1/125 | Plus X Acutol | −Normal |
| 119 | Bronica | 50 | 8 | 1/30 | Plus X Acufine | Normal |
| 121 | Bronica | 250 | 6:3 | 1/60 | Plus X Acutol | −Normal |

| Page | Camera | Lens | Stop F. Number | Shutter Speed | Film and Developer | Time + or − Normal |
|------|--------|------|----------------|---------------|--------------------|--------------------|
| 123 | Bronica | 135 | 11 | 1/125 | Plus X Acutol | +Normal |
| 125 | Bronica | 135 | 9 | 1/125 | Plus X Acutol | −Normal |
| 127 | Bronica | 135 | 9 | 1/125 | Plus X Acutol | −Normal |
| 130 | Bronica | 135 | 4 | 1/30 | Plus X Acutol | Normal |
| 137 | Bronica | 50 | 11 | 1/25 | Plus X Acutol | Normal |
| 138 | Bronica | 50 | 11 | 1/25 | Plus X Acutol | −Normal |
| 147 | Bronica | 135 | 11 | 1/250 | Plus X Acutol | −Normal |
| 151 | Bronica | 50 | 11 | 1/60 | Plus X Acutol | −Normal |

## COLOUR

The colour pictures follow page 80.

1    The first colour picture is a photograph of the painting 'Bonnie Prince Charlie in 1745' by T. S. Evans. Both painting and photograph belong to the Drambuie Liqueur Co. Ltd.

| | Camera | Lens | F. Stop | Shutter Speed | Film |
|------|--------|------|---------|---------------|------|
| 2 | Bronica | 135 | 5·6 | 1/125 | Ektachrome X |
| 3 | Bronica | 50 | 11 | 1/60 | Ektachrome X |
| 4 | Bronica | 135 | 8 | 1/125 | Ektachrome X |
| 5 | Bronica | 135 | 4 | 1/30 | Ektachrome X |
| 6 | Bronica | 50 | 12·5 | 1/15 | Ektachrome X |
| 7 top | Bronica | 135 | 8 | 1/125 | Ektachrome X |
| 7 bottom | Bronica | 135 | 4 | 1/30 | Ektachrome X |
| 8 | Bronica | 50 | 11 | 1/60 | Ektachrome X |

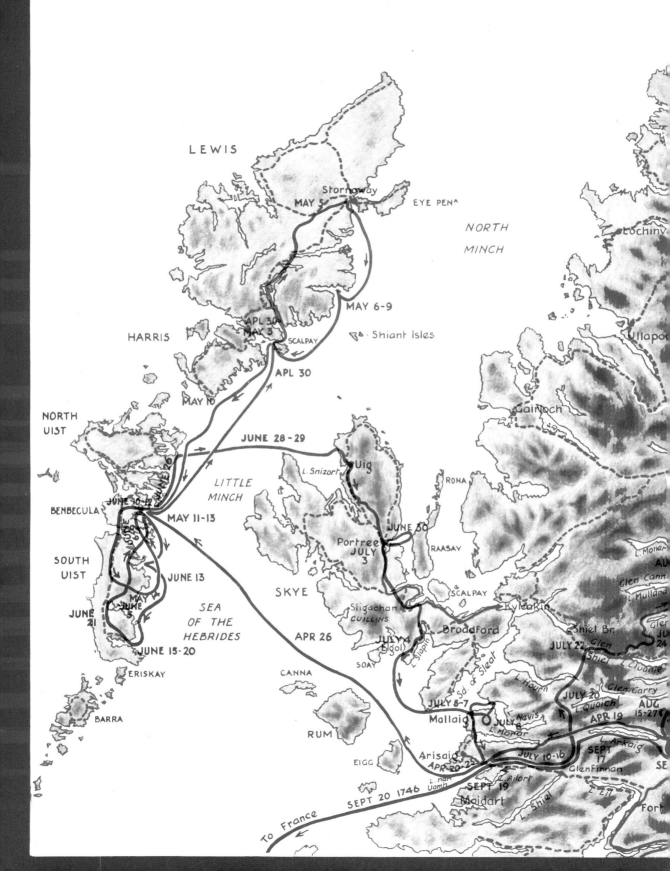